AVRIL BLAKE
The Design Council

Milner Gray

First edition published in the United Kingdom 1986 by
The Design Council
28 Haymarket
London SW1Y 4SU

Typeset by Sunrise Setting, Torquay, Devon

Printed by Raithby Lawrence, Leicester

British Library CIP Data
Blake, Avril
  Milner Gray.
  1. Gray, Milner
  I. Title   II. Design Council
  745.2′092′4   TS140.G7/

ISBN 0 85072 158 X

Contents

Milner Gray.

Introduction

Anyone can be wise after the event. Studying Milner Gray's career, it is obvious that the whole reason for his success was that he was wise before the event, with an astute perception of what the market would be by the time his design came before the public eye. This sensitivity may have had its origin in his not being physically strong enough to endure the rigours of much formal schooling. 'I've always enjoyed weak health' he has cheerfully said of himself at the age of 85. 'I was thought to be sickly. In fact people thought I wouldn't survive.'

And so, exempt from school for many months at a time, he pursued his own ideas and interests and gained from this an individuality and quality of judgement that have remained throughout his life.

Without sufficient formal schooling, he lacked qualification for an academic career and was therefore sent to Goldsmiths' College, London University, at the age of 16. Here he studied in the schools of painting, etching and design.

In 1917 be became eligible for military service and was posted to the 19th London Regiment. However, his weak health saved his life for, after training at Aldershot, his medical category was lowered and, instead of going to France with his battalion, which was decimated, he was transferred to the experimental section of the Royal Engineers' School of Camouflage.

On leaving the school, Milner Gray was one of the first to recognise that, despite the many organisations which had been created during the 19th century to improve the standard of British industrial goods, a division between artist and manufacturer had somehow grown up. Only in Germany and America (where Norman Bel Geddes is credited as being the first to adopt the term 'industrial designer' in 1927) did manufacturers and designers catch on to the idea of working together to design for industry. In Britain, the great names of those thought to be 'designers' in the early years of the century were, in fact, usually independent freelance artists. However, after the First World War, a lot of their work was taken over by firms of advertising agents who organised regular campaigns based on market research.

Gray saw that many modern designing tasks were beyond the powers of individual artists working alone, and were better tackled by a small group of diverse specialists working together on a more or less equal footing. To this end, he joined with Charles and Henry Bassett to form the Bassett-Gray Studio in 1921. These three were joined by Jesse Collins, Colin Dilly, Bouverie Hoyton and Alan Rogers in the early 1920s and later acquired a group of associates including Graham Sutherland and Clive Gardiner. From this time onward, until the Second World War, Gray and his colleagues consistently maintained an output of well considered, distinguished drawings and designs, setting a standard which few artists of the period could equal.

Bassett-Gray was not the only product of Gray's enterprise and determination to better the designer's lot. In 1929 he got together with a few friends to discuss the setting up of a professional body for designers with the aim of improving their conditions, their fees and salaries, and their status in society. He has said of this, 'The only thing that I have done that I think will stand the test of time is the setting up of the SIAD in 1929–30.'

He has recalled:

'Many of our earlier meetings had been in the Cock Tavern in Fleet Street, which happened to be handy for several of us, but some specially vital ones had been held in Hock's – Lilian Hocknells' – studio in Flood Street, Chelsea, and others in a basement room of the old

Adelphi Hotel. Anyway, on that September morning we left a solicitor's office in the Strand having set our signatures to the memorandum and articles of association of the Society of Industrial Artists – the SIA, later to become the SIAD, was born. Eighteen days later, on 11 October, the Society was duly incorporated as a Company Limited by Guarantee and not having a share capital.

'There were ten of us on that momentous morning, all members of the original pre-formation committee: Lilian Hocknell, herself; Oliver Bernard; James Morton; Gordon Nichol; Harold Stabler; Septimus Scott and myself, who signed the document as subscribers, and Sir Herbert Morgan; R. P. Gosop; Comerford Watson and Harold Forster who were named in the Articles respectively as first President, Honorary Secretary and joint Honorary Treasurers. Others of the pre-formation group were Henry Coller and Fred Taylor.

'Sir Herbert Morgan, then a Director of the *Daily Telegraph*, had been Controller of W. H. Smith's printing department and responsible for organising the once famous studio of their advertising agency, to which he had recruited an outstanding company of graphic talent: Gossop had been studio director, and now, whilst continuing in private practice as a textile, wallpaper and graphic designer, also acted as an agent for other designers. Of the rest of us, seven were almost exclusively graphic artists, including myself at that time; Oliver Bernard described himself as an architect–decorator – he was responsible for the interior design of the recently opened Lyons Corner House; Harold Stabler was a silversmith, potter and heraldic designer and was Principal of the Sir John Cass School of Art; James Morton was the only signatory to style himself "designer" '[1]

Harold Stabler was also a Design and Industries Association founder member.

'Reactions of other professional bodies,' Milner Gray has said, 'were not very good at first; they thought we were rather radical. But we had sufficient influence to get recognition where it mattered, in the companies like Wedgewoods and so on.'

In 1935, the Bassett-Gray partnership was dissolved and re-formed as Industrial Design Partnership. This included Misha Black, who had joined Bassett-Gray in 1932.

Milner Gray's own work was, at first, that of an illustrator. He specialised in period subjects, using a conventional treatment for his figure drawings, with clear-cut pen-and-ink technique. In time, however, 'Gray the cloak-and-sword illustrator', as George Butler, art director of the J. Walter Thompson Company once called him, 'gave place to Gray the designer.'[2]

He always had a strong sense of what was contemporary in design and was one of the first to recognise the value of the German school of lettering and design for printing, which had reached such refinement in the years after the First World War. The work of Hadank and Koch, particularly, made a deep impression on Milner Gray in the early '30s. It was work which emphasised immaculate craftsmanship and a respect for tradition (the woodcut always in the background) and this has been the hallmark of Milner Gray's designs throughout his career. Some of Gray's best work of this period was shown in his bottle designs: simple forms, hand-shaped in origin, the label cut in a flattened oval and the design in scrollwork.

All the same, some years before the Second World War, Milner Gray was, once again, one of the first to realise that the industrial artist ought to extend his work to mass produced design, in addition to the craft-based industries, packaging and advertising. At that time new

German teachers from the Bauhaus were coming to England where many of their ideas were sympathetically received. The teaching of the Bauhaus faced up to the problems of designing for mass production and the slogans describing this ('Form follows function' and 'Truth to materials') were great debating points within the design profession. Gray made good use of all these ideas without ever losing the essential Englishness of his own work.

The second World War interrupted this work, but Milner Gray was able to continue working in his own field when he was made Head of the exhibitions branch of the Ministry of Information. Here he had to start from scratch to build up the department, collecting together a team of artists and craftsmen who designed and constructed exhibitions for display in many parts of the country.

In 1942, however, at a time when it still seemed doubtful enough whether England would win the war, let alone go back to normal living, Milner Gray was asked by Cecil D. Notley, then Head of Notley Advertising, who had been having discussions with Marcus Brumwell (Chairman and Managing Director of Stuart's Advertising Agency) and Herbert Read for a detailed plan for the kind of design service that Gray felt would be needed when the war was over. He put forward a paper outlining proposals for a design unit based on a further development of his pre-war design partnership, IDP. His plans were adopted and Design Research Unit came into being; but Notley later withdrew and Brumwell, Black and Gray became the three founder partners.

The list of Milner Gray's achievements after the Second World War is formidable. Apart from running the practice, working as a teacher, writer and occasional lecturer, helping to expand the SIAD and sitting on innumerable committees and boards, his design work continued to flourish. It included bottles, packaging, coats of arms, signposting for the Festival of Britain, china and oven-to-tableware, corporate identity programmes, exhibitions, the ship's badge for the 'Oriana' (for which he was also joint co-ordinating designer with Misha Black and Kenneth Bayes for the interior design), and the emblem for the Queen's Silver Jubilee.

Even so, this Introduction only presents the facts of Milner Gray's lifetime when the reality has been far more than bleakly factual. Leaving art school for the First World War, building up a business through the '20s and '30s slump, having to wind up his business for another war, starting once again in 'the age of austerity', Milner Gray, weak health and all, generated a sense of fun and enthusiasm that was caught, echoed and appreciated by clients, colleagues, committee members and delegates at SIAD and ICSID conferences.

He believed that this light touch, this underlying good humour, was good business and an essential for designers whose bright creative imagery could not flourish in an atmosphere in any way touched by 'the dead hand of blight'.

'I'm very optimistic,' he said to Jane Lott, who interviewed him for DESIGN magazine in June 1982. 'The role of design in the world is growing stronger. The need to understand it is being appreciated by engineers'. The author hopes to catch something of this optimism and its resulting inspiration to other designers in the pages of this book.

Cyril Hart Campbell Gray, Doris Katherine Vicat Gray and Milner Connorton Gray, in about 1901.

Gray's father, Archibald Campbell Gray.

Gray's mother, Katherine May Gray, née Hart.

Gray of Bassett-Gray

Family

The best design has a timeless quality and Milner Gray's work, throughout his long career, has always had the timeless quality of traditional craftsmanship. He was born in 1899 into a world of seemingly absolute values, a world which was shattered in 1914 when only frail health saved him from dying, like millions of other young men, in the First World War.

Milner Connorton Gray was the second son and second child of Archibald Campbell Gray and Katherine May Gray, née Hart. He was born at Blackheath, with two brothers, Cyril Hart Campbell Gray and Thomas Archibald Campbell Gray, and two sisters, Doris Katherine Vicat Gray and Margaret Hamilton Gray.

In a light-hearted talk to the Arts Club which he introduced as 'I Think I Remember', Milner Gray recalled:

'In 1899 the old Queen was still on the throne ruling a now departed Empire; dear Albert, of whom it was somewhat ungratefully said that he had a great deal of taste and all of it bad, was but a revered memory. A clear starlit night heralded a bright autumnal day in early October when I was born in Blackheath on the outskirts of London, but frankly I don't remember anything of it. The war in South Africa was to drag on from that October until May 1902, but it meant absolutely nothing to me.

'I do remember weeping at an early age on the horrid realisation that I was growing older and, whilst the habit has somehow persisted, for better or worse I have put the thought of it from me ever since.

'I remember the handsome artilleryman in Greenwich Park, magnificent in his "blues", who, in answer to my timid enquiry about the time, relayed by my nursemaid, replied, with an eye on the nursemaid and not on the clock, "It's ten past kissing time, time to kiss again . . ."

'I vividly recall, despite the passage of time, standing horrified, yet enthralled, at the sight of our baker thrown from the van by his runaway horse and lying bleeding and unconscious in the roadway.

'I remember kneeling decently at morning prayers, and the maids in their stiff blue morning frocks piously presenting their posteriors to the Almighty, rather shyly perhaps for they were plump, yet peeping somewhat less shyly between their fingers, conscious that they were sticking out behind.

'I remember riding in one of the last of the horse-drawn trams in Woolwich; my grandfather's Victoria which, when we were lucky, took us to church on a Sunday morning; Thomas Tilling's horse buses; the unforgettable smell and creak of the hackney cab and, later, the "handsome" before King Edward and his motor and World War One all but swept them away.'[3]

Blackheath as it was at this time has been described by Dorothy McCall, a friend of Milner Gray's mother:

'Over Blackheath we drove; past the Princess of Wales' Pond and Rotten Row, occasionally dodging a stray golf ball, for men in scarlet jackets still pursued the Royal and Ancient game on King James' original links, despite the increasing maze of roads and cricket pitches through which they must thread their way . . .'[4]

'We had generally what is described as a Christian upbringing: my father's family were Presbyterian, my grandfather (who came to England from the west coast of Scotland by way of Edinburgh) being a clergyman in the Church of Scotland. My mother's family were Baptists and, as children, we generally attended the Baptist church at Lee, where my grandfather maintained a family pew. We could hardly be described as sectarian for we also attended the Presbyterian Church in Greenwich or the Anglican Church in Blackheath as the mood might take us – or the inclination to walk across the Heath. A member of the church congregation at Lee was a most distinguished figure with long, white dundrearies: Sir Nathanial Barnaby, designer of the first dreadnoughts. As children our proper behaviour on Sundays was encouraged by the cautionary dictum "Today is Sunday, the Sabbath day, and we must neither work nor play, nor run about nor make a noise, like naughty little girls and boys." Bound volumes of *The Sunday and Home* were permitted to be read. *The Strand Magazine* was also permitted on weekdays.'

The children heard their parents refer to Sir Nathanial as 'Sir Nat', but this created in their young minds the much more intriguing suggestion that this was 'Sir Gnat' and, says Gray, 'We wondered if he had a sting'.

When Gray reached school age, he was sent to Belmont, a nearby preparatory school in Blackheath Village where he was given a good grounding in the usual subjects and played cricket and hockey. From here he went to Colfe Grammar School in Lewisham where, at first, he was well ahead of the other children in knowledge. However, bad health began to keep him away from school for months at a time and he lost ground as a scholar. Even so, he won three prizes for general proficiency, these being books

The Gray family, in about 1912.

which, he now says cheerfully, held no interest for him whatsoever. He has recalled, 'I was batted from one school to another, being a sickly child, and only began to find my feet when, in desperation, my parents sent me to art school.'[5]

This was the school attached to Goldsmith's College, London University, where he studied under Stanley Anderson and Malcolm Osborn (who both taught engraving); Edmund J. Sullivan (who had illustrated Omar Kayam and Carlisle's *French Revolution*); and Harold Speed (a society portrait painter noted for a full length portrait of Edward VII). At Goldsmiths', Gray gained an LCC scholarship, although he has said that he felt, at the time, that he was far from being their greatest scholar. 'I much preferred,' he has confessed, 'going off to play tennis or to flirt with the girls.'

In the early years of the war, Milner joined the junior London Scottish cadet battalion, hoping to be accepted by the parent regiment, but when the time came he failed to meet the physical requirements, as he did, again, for the RF Corps, Inns of Court, City of London Yeomanry, and the Honourable Artillery Company. For a brief spell he worked in a munitions factory but, on his call-up, was then posted to the 19th London Regiment. This was in 1917 and he was given three months' training at Aldershot and Blackdown but was prevented from going to France with the battalion when his health category was lowered. At the front, the battalion was virtually wiped out. Gray was finally transferred to the Royal Engineers' experimental section school of camouflage stationed in Hyde Park until he was demobilised in 1919.

The setting up of Bassett-Gray

When he was demobilised, Milner Gray went back to Goldsmith's College as a student. Charles Bassett was also there again, having seen service in France with the Horse Artillery. Charles had a brother, Henry, and their father, Edward, was a lecturer who had an office in Imperial Buildings, Ludgate Circus. After leaving Goldsmiths' in 1921, Milner Gray formed a partnership with Charles and Henry Bassett, the 'Bassett-Gray Group of Artists and Writers'. This was situated in an office at the foot of Fleet Street, next door to Edward Bassett, where they worked mostly for advertising agencies, publishers or printers.

The group was extended when the three founder partners were joined by other ex-students from Goldsmiths, Jesse Collins, Colin N. Dilly and, later, William Larkins, originally an engraver. Gradually others also joined, including Alan Martin-Harvey who had been at Colfe Grammar School with Gray and was a partner with his father, an advertising consultant, from whom Bassett-Gray received many early commissions. As an associate of Bassett-Gray, Alan Martin-Harvey wrote much of their copy. Milner has said about this:

'In 1921, I left art school and set up in practice in Ludgate Circus with one or two fellow students to earn my living in the world of advertising. Those were the days of the rhyming slogan: "Over the fence leaps Sunny Jim, Force is the food that raises him", or "Prompted by that Kruschen feeling, Grandpa raced the train to Ealing"; or the one I liked the best: "Better than all your fur lined coats are stomachs lined with Plasmon Oats".'[6]

Bassett-Gray was the first multi-discipline design practice of its kind in England and described itself as 'the distributing organisation of a body of artists who design for industrial and commercial purposes'. A brochure at the time reads: 'The members of Bassett-Gray, being convinced that it must be to your advantage to deal from the first with creative artists, practised in advertising, have decided to place the sole representation of the Group in the hands of William Martin Larkins, ARE, and Milner Gray, to one or other of whom all enquiries in future should be addressed'.

Commercial Art magazine in December 1927, published a short article which stated:

'The Bassett-Gray is an efficient organisation founded some four years ago by Mr Charles Bassett and Mr Milner Gray and composed of a number of freelance artists and writers who work together. From small beginnings, it is rapidly developing into a considerable enterprise.

'The founders have been joined by a number of colleagues who desire to steer a middle course between the stultifying influence of the commercial art factory on the one hand and the limited opportunities of complete isolation on the other.

'From the beginning, certain definite ideals have been set and strictly adhered to. Each member of the Bassett-Gray group is an individual craftsman, drawing inspiration from his own sources, working on his own individual lines and freely developing his individual style.'

The arrangement of the company left everyone free to come and go and worked well. It was a venture in tune with the times; 'flexibility' had to remain the key to success in making design a recognisable profession. However, in the 1920s, design was not a recognisable profession at all. Designers were mere 'commercial artists, letterers or draughtsmen', skilled craftsmen rather than professional people and very poorly paid for the work they did. Nevertheless a start had been made on the way towards a reformation.

Gray at work in 1924 (aged 25).

Bassett-Gray and Industrial Design Partnership

Social Activities

In his private life, after the First World War, Milner Gray left his parents' home to take 'digs' on his own, not far away, in a Queen Anne house at 2 Grotes Place, Blackheath. Here he rented a bedroom and a sitting room for a year or two before Graham Sutherland, looking for similar accommodation, took one of the other bedrooms at Grotes Place and shared Milner's sitting room with him.

At this time Milner joined the HAC for a chance to go horse riding, and his tendency, after this, to turn up in the office in riding dress caused his teasing partners and associates to label him 'Hunting Crop Gray'.

This cheerful recognition of the need for 'play' as well as 'work' extended to devising an annual treat for Bassett-Gray clients – an annual dinner that included a light-hearted ceremony called 'The Bibbing of Patrons'. These dinners were attended by the corporate and associate members of the group practice, by invited clients (particularly in the advertising world) and by patrons and VIPs (including Royal Academicians).

The 1927 ceremony was described by an article in *Advertising world* under the title 'Art Dines with Commerce'. This said:

'Is the immensely higher standard of commercial art which prevails to-day gradually helping the advertiser, by more and more insistent appeals to the public imagination, to sell the public machine-made goods to saturation point — thus slowly completing a cycle which will, in time, take us back to the more costly products of the craftsman, exquisitely and with infinite labour made by hand?

'This interesting theory was advanced by Harold Speed at the Fourth Annual Dinner of the Bassett-Gray group of artists, held at "Ye Olde Dr Butler's Head" on September 9. The occasion was that of the bibbing of patrons by this peculiar organisation of united freelancers in all branches of commercial art.'

Graham Sutherland and Paul Drury were both 'bibbed' on this occasion and Paul Drury presented two masers or loving cups to the proceedings – one christened the She-cup and the other the He-cup.

The Advertisers' Weekly of the following year described that year's studio dinner as:

'A high-spirited and wholly unusual kind of advertising dinner . . . The occasion was the

'Hunting Crop' Gray, October 1930 (aged 31).

fifth "Bibbing of Patrons", a ceremony conducted with facetious solemnity, a Latin service and in mock-mediaeval setting heightened by the gorgeous raiment and colourful bibs of members of the studio.

'"Commerce, literature and graphic art" was the subject of the toast proposed by Mr Alan Martin-Harvey on this occasion, to which Mr Charles Tomkinson responded in the name of commerce, Mr W. Haslam Mills for literature and Mr Edmund J. Sullivan for graphic art.'

This mixture of entertainment and business was a great success. Bassett Gray went on from strength to strength unaffected by the Wall Street Crash in 1929 which did, however, knock the bottom out of the etchings market in which Graham Sutherland and Paul Drury had been doing well. One result of this was that Graham Sutherland turned to painting and accepted commissions for posters, publicity, ceramics and fabrics, much of which work was channelled through Bassett-Gray.

Milner Gray showed some of Sutherland's work to Jack Beddington, Shell's advertising director, and this led to the commissioning of a poster for Shell based on a Sutherland etching 'Near Leeds, Kent', showing two oast houses in

Christmas card for the Bassett-Gray Studio, 1925.

Bassett-Gray dinner menu of 1925. Designed by Alan Rogers and depicting his own face, Milner Gray's, Charles and Henry Bassett's, Colin Dilly's and Alan Martin Harvey (in a bowler hat).

Bassett-Gray dinner menu of 1926. Designed by Eric Fraser, depicting Bouverie Hoyton as Durer's 'Nemesis' (photo alongside). Bassett-Gray staff are on the right, patrons on the left.

a silvan setting. The original gouache for this still hangs in Shell-Mex house.

Graham Sutherland also changed his way of life. He left the 'digs' he shared with Milner Gray and, on 29 December 1927, married Kathleen Barry, another ex-Goldsmiths' student and went to live in Farningham in Kent.

Milner Gray, however, remained in Blackheath which was convenient for meeting designer friends in London. They were convinced that the status of the designer must be raised to that of a recognised profession. Without such recognition they felt that the designer would never get the necessary support from the industrialist to enable him to play a more constructive and responsible part in improving the appearance of artefacts. They therefore discussed ways of bettering their lot and, by 1929, began to meet regularly to consider setting up a professional body which could fight their battles for them.

Of this Milner Gray wrote in his preface to *Minerva at Fifty*:

'. . . it now seems a very far cry to those preformation meetings in The Cock Tavern in Fleet Street when those few of us that there then were argued our way towards a formal constitution, or to those later meetings in a basement

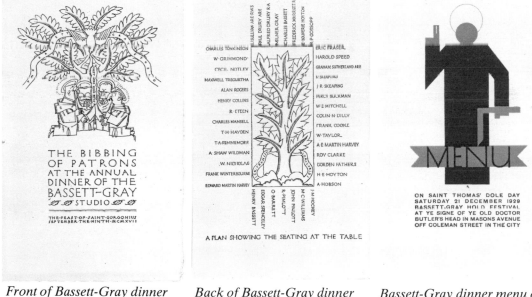

Front of Bassett-Gray dinner menu of 1927. Designed by Eric Fraser and showing Edmund J. Sullivan, Frederick Marriott, R. P. Gossop and Alfred Drury (kneeling).

Back of Bassett-Gray dinner menu of 1927.

Bassett-Gray dinner menu of 1929. Designed by Alan Rogers.

HORNE

Bassett-Gray dinner, 1927.

room in the now departed Adelphi Hotel, when we had welded ourselves into a corporate body and laid the foundations for a continuing programme of developments . . .

'In those early days, apart from the very few, the attitude of manufacturers, distributors and indeed of the general public to design and designers was one of unconscious indifference; and consequently the average conditions of employment of designers and the scale of remuneration for design services were, by today's standards, deplorably low. Such designers as there were, and they were far fewer in number than they are today, were working in isolation and, generally speaking, were looked at askance by industry.

'Over the years the practice of design, in common with the development of industry as a whole, has witnessed a period of considerable change. New technologies have imposed new constraints as well as setting new horizons and we all face problems created by working with or in the areas affected by continuing technological and social change.'[7]

Misha Black joins Bassett-Gray

In 1929, Charles Bassett decided to leave the Bassett-Gray partnership and go to Odhams as a copywriter. The following year the design group had the chance to move to larger offices on the top floor of 4 Bedford Square. However, Henry Bassett decided to remain in private practice in the old offices.

Milner Gray now took charge of Bassett-Gray and kept it going, without changing the name of the firm. His work at this time included book jackets, illustrations, a press advertisement for the South African Wines Company, advertisements for Balkan Sobranie, and advertising and a stand for BP. It was in connection with his work for BP that Gray first met his life-long partner, Misha Black, in 1932.

'I was talking to Joan Saxon-Mills, a director of Cummings Advertising, with whom we were dealing,' Gray can remember, 'when Misha, who was then working for Arundell Display, came in with a huge model of a stand for BP. He was almost hidden by it.' Since William Larkins had just left Bassett-Gray to go to J. Walter

Bassett-Gray writing paper with a range of headings, early 1930s.

Bassett-Gray card setting out their services in about 1932. Designed by Gray.

Thomson, Bassett-Gray were short-handed on display skills. Gray was impressed by Black's work and offered him a job, which was accepted enthusiastically.

In the same year Milner Gray became a member of the visiting staff at Goldsmiths' College, the Chelsea School of Art and the Reimann School of Art and Design. At the Reimann School, where Austin Cooper was Principal, Milner Gray taught styling, packaging and advertisement design, posts which he held until the first year of the Second World War. He also acted as one of the design co-ordinators for the commercial art section of the advertising and marketing exhibition at Olympia in London in 1933, and exhibited a number of printed textile designs at the exhibition of British Industrial Art at Dorland Hall, London.

Frank Yearbury also put Milner Gray's name forward as a designer of a promotional scheme to launch the London Building Centre and Gray designed a symbol, a poster and a series of press advertisements for this.

Poster for the London Building Centre designed by Gray as part of a promotional scheme to launch the Centre in 1930.

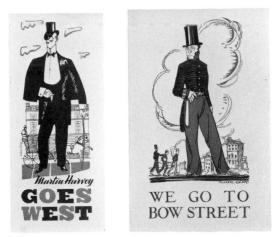

Two change of address cards for the Martin Harvey Advertising Service, designed by Milner Gray, one about 1925 ('We Go To Bow Street') and the other about 1953.

Industrial Design Partnership

Gray now began to extend his own work from graphic design to product design, designing china and pottery for two firms, E. Brain & Co. and Royal Staffordshire Pottery, to both of whom he was appointed design consultant.

In 1935, the Bassett-Gray group practice was dissolved and re formed under the new name of Industrial Design Partnership. This change was perhaps best described by S. L. Righyni in *The Boxmakers' Journal and Packaging Review*:

'The group handle complete schemes of presentation, from the styling of goods to the press advertising. Packaging has a great part in the organisation of these schemes and has brought the group respect and sometimes distinction. The complete approach has been built up: materials, designs, construction and costs are studied. The group is equipped, through its research and the specialised knowledge of one or several of its members, to give intelligent assistance and a guidance to any firm that sees the value of a good pack in the selling scheme . . .'

This article was illustrated with, amongst other things, soap and packaging designed by Jesse Collins for the Blind Institute; Kappa Rice packs designed by Milner Gray for C. T. Bowring; wine jars in imitation salt glaze for the mid-Sussex Canning and Preserving Company, also designed by Milner Gray; and china for E. Brain & Co., designed by Milner Gray and Graham Sutherland.

It is interesting to note this first mention of 'research' in this publicity. Research was to be a service more and more strongly emphasised in this context. And, of course, Gray's third design group was to be called Design Research Unit.

Bassett-Gray had taught Milner Gray that there were two stages in the solving of design problems: the second was the personal, intuitive

Gray's illustration, text and typography for a press advertisement for Balkan Sobranie cigarettes in about 1927.

creation of the drawing or artefact; the first, equally important, was analytical and objective – finding out what the manufacturer and the public wanted as a product. For this it was necessary for the designer to 'research', to ask questions and to find out which were the right questions to ask. Gray built up a checklist of questions which he extended over the years to cover the ever wider range of projects and products. He said, of this process:

'The design process advances by a procession of mental images which are tested and accepted and rejected. Each image, even the least valuable, may be used as a progenitor for variants

'Mayfair' tea service designed by Gray for E. Brain & Co. in 1933–4. Produced in white bone china decorated by offset transfer from copper plate engravings.

Packs designed by Gray during the 1930s for Bryantson biscuits.

and for other new images. The mechanism of design, therefore, requires a stream of ideas either directly from initial concepts or, more commonly, budding, developing, mutating rapidly and prolifically from one another. The basis of conceptual thinking grows from a background of accumulated experience, a collected fund of observed facts about the job which, for the moment, we might leave to one side but which, at the *right* moment, and with the appropriate stimulus, we will recall and find the solutions to the problems posed. Data alone will not provide the answer, but data is still necessary. Design is a process of analysis, synthesis and genesis. The designer has a great social responsibility, for no-one else is likely to be so much concerned with the real total value of the product to its ultimate user.'

IDP included among its clients Kodak and Hartley's for packaging; Ekco for radio cabinets; the Gas Light and Coke Company for room heaters and exhibitions; and Kardomah Cafes for shop design. Milner Gray designed

Interior of a flat at Blackheath, designed by Milner and Thomas Gray in about 1934. The curtain fabric and rug were designed by Gray, as were some Foley china that matched the curtain with a decoration in silver lustre.

murals and decorative features for Kardomah cafes in London, Birmingham and Manchester. He also designed hammock principle domestic chairs for Christie-Tyler in 1937 and acted as section designer, with Misha Black, for the MARS exhibition of modern architecture in London in 1938.

Other strands of Milner Gray's life at this time were interwoven with developments at IDP.

In 1934, he married Gnade Osborn Pratt. It was a quiet wedding at Christ Church, Mayfair, with Paul Drury as best man and Milner's sister Margaret as Gnade's bridesmaid. The bride and groom spent their honeymoon in Storrington in West Sussex at the White Hart Hotel, returning to live in Meadow Cottage, Eynsford, a few hundred yards away from the Sutherlands' Willow Cottage. Meadow Cottage, however, soon proved to be impractical.

Gray had more and more evening work for the art schools and the SIA and the couple moved to Hampstead so that he should not have such a long journey late at night. 'Gnade', Milner Gray has said, 'from the moment of our marriage, became a "technical college widow".'

He also continued to do a great deal of work for the Society of Industrial Artists. In 1935, for example, the SIA had produced a further declaration of policy which appeared in its annual report. This made the following points:

Gnade and Milner Gray at Honorable Artillery Company 'B' Battery Ball in 1934.

1   The future of the creative industrial artist and designer lies in his attaining professional status as in the case of the architect, the engineer, the solicitor, the surgeon, etc.

2   When he is employed in a professional capacity, he should be capable of taking, and should be accorded by industry, executive authority and responsibility such as is at present accorded to the works manager, the sales manager, the engineer, etc. Alternatively, as a 'freelance', he should take the same position in relation to industry as the consultant.

3   To be fitted to fill such positions, he must have wide general knowledge and experience, and a full grasp of the technical and commercial problems of the industries in which he operates.

4   The Society of Industrial Artists Ltd. will take steps to ensure that all new entrants into the profession through membership of the Society have these views and their corresponding responsibilities clearly put before them.

5 The Society of Industrial Artists Ltd. will endeavour to lay down standards to ensure that membership of the Society carries a guarantee of adequate academic, artistic, technical and commercial qualifications and to establish a code of professional conduct binding on its members.

6 The Society of Industrial Artists Ltd. will co-operate with educational authorities to ensure that suitable and adequate educational facilities are made available to prospective entrants into the profession and with every industry which is prepared to take its share of responsibility for the absorption of a proportion of new entrants at a proper remuneration and with proper conditions of employment.

James Holland has written, of this period:

'In general terms it can be claimed that the society's history reflects its close adherence to the policies then laid down. However, the character of a newly founded organisation will derive not only from its declared aims but also from its day-to-day activities in pursuit of those aims, not only from the 39 articles but also from the church fete. On this evidence the embryo society amounted to a select group of artists, designers and craftsmen – later becoming several groups – meeting regularly and convivially to discuss the pursuit of their stated aims and to listen to lecturers and discourses by colleagues and guest speakers. My earliest personal recollection of encountering the SIA is of a friendly evening of talk, darts and bitter in a south London pub, a tweedy, pipe-smoking occasion much in keeping with the character of that pre-war decade.

'A list of the officers and Council for 1932–33 is impressive:

President and Council Chairman
Paul Nash
Vice-Chairman
P. H. Jowett
Council
C. F. Angrave, Serge Chermayeff FRIBA
Austin Cooper, Frank Dobson
Frederick Etchells FRIBA
Lilian Hocknell, A. S. Knight, W. M.
Larkins, Denham MacLaren, G. E. Ridout
Graham Sutherland, G. A. Wade
J. Wadsworth, Allan Walton
Joint Hon. Treasurers
Comerford Watson, G. W. Leech
Joint Hon. Secretaries
Freda Lingstrom, Milner Gray

'What may strike us most about this list is the number of distinguished "fine artists" then actively involved with the society. Paul Nash, Frank Dobson, Graham Sutherland and Allan Walton were perhaps the best known, but many others were also well known both as artists and designers.

'Almost as striking is the comparative absence of industrial product designers, an imbalance that it was to take many years to remedy . . .'[9]

Holland also wrote:

'In its pre-war period, the society had valuable contacts with other bodies concerned with design. The Design and Industries Association – the DIA – was rather senior in foundation to the SIA, and though its objectives were not directly concerned with the status of the professional designer, it shared many of the society's aims affecting the quality of British industrial design. During 1933 and 1934, the SIA had been considering closer links between the various voluntary organisations that existed to serve both the designer and the manufacturer, with the intention of avoiding energy-dissipating overlaps, and at the DIA's suggestion a joint committee was set up to implement this. The society was also considering moving its headquarters to be under the same roof as the DIA – a state of co-habitation eventually to be achieved at Carlton House Terrace.'[10]

Early headquarters of the society were in the Architectural Association's premises in Bedford Square and later moved to Queen Anne's Gate. The society was then temporarily housed with the Honorary Treasurer and many

of its earliest records were lost through bombing. Those that survived were given into the custody of the North Staffordshire branch, and this Midlands group did much to keep the society in a state of continuing, if suspended, existence during the war years.

Many of the SIA's earlier members were also closely involved in the activities of the AIA, the Artists' International Association, which had come into being in the early '30s to channel the anti-fascist anti-war feelings manifest among artists of all aesthetic persuasions and practices into the most effective form. AIA was an organi-

Salt glazed stoneware jar with an engraved label; designed by Gray. Part of a range of country wines produced for the mid-Sussex Canning and Preserving Company.

Bone china decorations for Foley China (E. Brain & Co). Top three by Milner Gray, bottom two by Graham Sutherland.

sation essentially for its time and its time was the '30s and the war years. The history of the association ran its own course and cannot be followed here, but much of its considerable impact in the critical years was planned and carried through by a number of designers including Misha Black, James Boswell, Lynton Lamb, Henrion, James Fitton and others who were to bring their experience and skills to the re-development of the SIA in the post-war years.

Milner Gray was both a member of the AIA and the DIA, becoming a Council member of the latter in 1935. In 1937 he was appointed Head of the Sir John Cass School of Art as well as supervising the design and craft classes. He also introduced a close contact between the art and design department and the metallurgy and engineering department, purchasing presses and other equipment jointly for use by both departments. A link with the Royal Mint was also established, by which their engraving apprentices studied at the school.

The Advertiser's Weekly for 5 August 1937, and *Art and Industry* for August 1937, both announced this appointment, the latter stating,

'Mr Gray is a practising designer – his chairmanship of Industrial Design Partnership is will known and in this field of teaching he will probably find an opportunity for extending to students his experience in producing design for mass-production.'

In 1938, Gray was elected a Royal Designer for Industry and the *Advertiser's Weekly* for 7 July 1938, ran the headline 'Five new Royal Designers for Industry appointed by the RSA'.

During 1938 and 1939, Milner Gray acted as Chairman of the SIA working party to consider the setting of examinations in design and the granting of qualifying diplomas, and from 1939 to 1940 he was a member of the visiting staff of the Royal College of Art.

Packaging design

At this time he wrote and read a paper on *'The History and Development of Packaging'* to the Royal Society of Arts in London. In this he said, 'Today, to the designer, to the advertising agent and to the packing industry, the work "packaging" has come to denote the art and science of packing merchandise to increase its sales, and it is to a brief examination of the history of this recent development, with something perhaps of the earlier background sketched in, that I invite your attention this evening.'

He then examined the history of packaging from the invention of paper in China, through glass bottles in Egypt, Greece and Rome, and cosmetic pots in Pompeii, to contemporary packaging including some examples of his own work. He also said:

'Design is intention, purpose, plan. When I say I have done a thing designedly, I mean that I have done this thing with a purpose. I have conceived a mental plan of what I have intended to do and have carried out that plan. This plan and its execution may, of course, be either good or bad. It may be a good plan well carried out or ill carried out; or it may be ill-conceived yet well executed. However well or ill, its conclusion, nevertheless, has been preconceived . . .

'The designer's first concern is to collect and collate the information on which his design will be constructed. He will ascertain the scope of the manufacturer's organisation and equipment for packing, the possibilities of its extension, the methods peculiar to his particular business.

'He will investigate the market for which the product is produced, assessing the relative value of the dressing of competitive lines. He will go into questions of practicability and economy of production, of appropriateness of colour, of harmony with the product, of legibility and attention value, of ease of handling of the pack

Silver porringer and spoon designed by Gray in 1937.

Kodak camera cartons. Two of a wide range of packings designed for this firm by Gray in the 1930s. The designs are in yellow, red and black.

in transit and on the dealer's shelves, questions of stacking and of mass patterning for purposes of display. Every package has to serve the purpose of advertising the product it contains everywhere it goes in the window, on the counter, in transit, on the dealers' shelf and in the consumer's cupboard. It should be legible and distinctive, an expression of the product that it contains. It should be recognisable immediately and, if possible, should be easily describable.'

In these years, just before the Second World War, packaging provided new opportunities for designers, calling for many of the skills and the attitude of mind required in the field of product design. Milner Gray designed many packages for foodstuffs, including biscuit packs, a mushroom pack, jelly cartons, cereal packs and custard powder packs. He also designed murals and decorations for the maritime section, and was responsible for a fine woollens section, of the British Pavilion at the New York World Fair. This, however, was in 1939.

Fear of war made houses begin to come onto the market because people were leaving London, and the Grays were able to buy their present home, Holly Mount, to which they moved. But war did come and miserably, frustratingly, just when Industrial Design Partnership was beginning to be known, it had to be disbanded.

The War Years

Ministry of Information

'I am now down to the last £10 I have been able to beg, borrow or steal,' Misha Black wrote to Milner Gray in November 1940, waiting to hear whether he, as a Russian, could join the British army.

Gray, however, had been suggested by Frank Pick and Kenneth Clark as Head of a Ministry of Information exhibitions branch and, in this position, he was able to gather together some of his old team, especially the European designers including Misha Black.

The Ministry of Information exhibitions branch, later re-titled the 'Display and Exhibitions' division,[11] was formed in November 1940, over a year after the official formation of the Ministry of Information. It was first housed on the ground floor of Senate House, the London University building in Mallet Street in an area partitioned off from the main entrance hall. In 1942, however, it was moved to Russell Square.

The new exhibitions branch was created under the direction of Milner Gray. The official war artists branch[12] was also split off from the main general production division of the Ministry of Information at the same time, the intention being that Kenneth Clark should run them both as a joint division. In practice, the nature of their work was so essentially different that the two branches co-existed rather than co-operated, and the exhibitions branch was always quite separate as far as its production was concerned.

The idea of using the exhibition as a propaganda vehicle seems to have been that of Frank Pick[13] who was Director General of the MoI from April until his resignation[14] in December 1940, a few months before his death. Pick, with his wide experience of publicity in all its forms, was undoubtedly aware of the relative value of each persuasive medium and had himself been an eager champion of the exhibition as a publicity tool, in his capacity as the controller of the underground's publicity for the London Passenger Transport Board. It is probably due to Pick's mediation that the MoI was able to capitalise on the few pre-war exhibition successes such as the use of the Charing Cross site and also the DIA's use of retail stores for travelling exhibitions.

The creation of the branch (later the division) was also born of a pressing need. The rapid expansion of publicity demands[15] during the first year of the war prompted the widening of the range of the MoI's publicity channels and the exhibition medium was an obvious addition to printed matter.

Gray was invited by Frank Pick to form an exhibitions branch because of his all-round graphic skills as a display, advertising and packaging designer. He was a natural, though interesting, choice for this role which he filled from 1940 to 1942, thereafter working as a part-time consultant until he left the division at the end of 1943. During these three years, he formed and directed the creative unit responsible for the MoI exhibitions and, at first, since he had no staff, it was know within the MoI as the 'one-man division'.[16] Gray, with his pre-war experience, was the knowledgeable link with professional exhibition designers in the commercial field, and it was his responsibility to gather his own staff. It is significant that in sharp contrast to the architecturally-biased exhibition personnel of pre-war days, this division (which concentrated on display techniques and played no part in exhibition building) should have been predominantly graphic in skills.

Gray was advised by A. W. Waterfield to draw upon the experienced exhibition staff of the GPO and the Department of Overseas Trade. However, no doubt mindful of their past creations, he responded with caution, stating that although the DOT '. . . would be employed as agents to carry out the work designed and planned by him and his staff . . . he did not think that either they or the GPO were likely to be able to produce anyone suitable.'[17]

With his wide experience, Gray here held the future of government exhibition in his hands and he sought to ensure that a civil service grew into something of broader significance. To this end, he was anxious to employ Misha Black, whom he regarded as the most talented individual practising in this field at the time. Notwithstanding Black's Russian origins and naturalisation problems,[18] Gray succeeded in arranging his employment from January 1941, on a weekly basis[19] as 'a constructive architect on the arrangement and layout of exhibitions, with special regard to his knowledge of propaganda requirements.'[20]

Since exhibition design was not a reserved occupation, Gray had some difficulty in accumulating a body of staff: architectural draughtsmen, for instance, were in short supply. Nevertheless, he succeeded in gathering together the following array of design talent.

Norbert Dutton, who was medically unfit, joined the exhibitions branch early on as a draughtsman and clerical assistant. Before the war he had formed Industrial Design Unit with Lonsdale Hands acting as its production director, and he was widely experienced in advertising agency practice and packaging, having been chief designer for the Metal Box Company for two years.

Peter Ray was similarly experienced in the graphic design field (then more commonly referred to as a commercial art) and was employed at first on a freelance basis, later becoming a full-time member of the design team as Head of the display section in charge of presentation and display. Ray was generally skilled in typography and book design, having been designer and production manager of the magazine *Shelf Appeal* before the war.

Other members of the design team were primarily experienced in the graphic and display design fields. Beverley Pick[21] who wrote a book on *Display Presentation* in 1947, was a German/Austrian refugee who had been successfully running a one-man window display business before the war. He became the head of the window display scheme when he joined the Ministry.

Gordon Cullen, who had been an architectural illustrator and writer, was employed in 1942 as a senior assistant designer on display and small exhibitions, with a specialism in pictorial statistics and display symbols.

Ronald Dickens who had previously been an exhibition designer, concentrated on displays and exhibitions, especially displays for overseas schemes.

James Holland, employed by the MoI in 1942, had previously been an artist/designer, involved in the AIA 'Artists Against Fascism' exhibition in 1935. Holland was one of the '3 James' of *Left Review*; James Boswell and James Fitton (also graphic designers) being the others. He worked on general displays and exhibitions, both at home and overseas.

Richard Levin, a freelance designer of exhibitions and general advertising, was employed as a senior designer for general display techniques in major exhibitions and was particularly interested and skilled in special lighting effects.

Kenneth Bayes, who had been with Gray before the war, was one of the few designers with an architectural background. He was employed as a senior designer for the major exhibitions, especially on the constructional side for temporary structures. Other architects were employed on a part-time basis for the more elaborate outdoor structural designs when needed. Those who joined the team which had escalated by 1943 from the original three to 64 designers were Tom Gentleman, a poster designer and W. Beechey, a typographer with printing experience. Charles Hasler and Bruce Roberts were appointed as display assistants and Elizabeth Craig as an architectural assistant.

In addition to this central core of permanent design staff, freelance designers were also widely used to supplement the work of the inside team, when it was over-worked or specialised techniques were required. At times the inside team functioned more as exhibition contractors for the occasional production of displays and models. The architects Ralph Tubbs, Frederick Gibberd, Bronek Katz, J. Berger and M. Baird, were used on an *ad hoc* basis, as were the designers F. H. K. Henrion, Lewitt-Him, Bruce Angrave, Jesse Collins and Pearl Faconer.[22]

From this list of personnel, it can be appreciated that Milner Gray made the most of so much talent which was available only because of the war. There had been no schools of exhibition design before the war and exhibition designers had therefore usually been trained as architects or commercial artists. Exhibitions were vehicles for propaganda and were judged by their merits for propaganda. This became especially true in wartime.

Within the beligerent countries, exhibitions had to build up morale, make more concrete a belief in the rightness of the cause for which the people were fighting, and give renewed confidence in the power to achieve victory. Sometimes they also had to deal with seemingly minor subjects such as persuading people to collect salvage, economise in food and essential supplies, work more and spend less, change their eating habits, leave their families, dig up their flower gardens and grow vegetables, and acquiesce in other generally disagreeable changes to their normal way of living.

In achieving these results it was impossible to separate the architectural and propagandist functions of the exhibition designer and, unless the designer was in complete sympathy with the propagandist attitude to the problem he could not produce a satisfactory result. The MoI exhibitions division developed a sympathetic attitude and a narrative formula which were so successful that they set the pace for all major exhibition designs in the western world after the war, notably for the Festival of Britain in 1951. The first essential for these exhibitions was a title which, when seen in the press and poster advertisements, excited people's curiosity sufficiently to make them come to the exhibition. Having got the public there, the first impression given was always sufficiently unusual to get the public to start walking round. The plan and visual emphasis would then lead the visitor to the main exhibition which was captioned with a narrative that explained whatever was aimed at by the exhibition itself. Facts were explained by, say, animated statistics and cold figures were humanised into a more easily understandable form. Finally, there would be encouragement to the visitor, who was sent away feeling educated and more hopeful.

The exhibitions division worked in close contact with other divisions of the Ministry such as the photographic division, the general production division, and the publications division in both consultative and practical ways. It also co-operated with the regional officers based around the country in the distribution of travelling displays. Other government departments involved in the staging of these exhibitions were HMSO for typesetting, block-making, printing and silk screening, and the Department of Overseas Trade for certain constructional jobs and the mounting of material.

SIMS LTD

The mural at the entrance to the Coal Hall, UK Pavilion, Empire exhibition, Glasgow in 1938.
The incised and colour-filled wood veneer panels were designed by Gray.

The Exhibitions

Once the permanent wartime exhibitions branch had been formed, the MoI staged numerous exhibitions in London, the provinces and abroad. In addition to one-off major exhibitions, travelling exhibitions (often based on the themes of major exhibitions) were circulated and also a retail display scheme was operated. The exhibitions varied in their approach but their scope ranged from exhibitions of an instructive, educational type such as 'Dig for Victory' and 'Poison Gas', morale boosters such as 'London Pride', and plainly propagandist exhibitions such as 'America Marches', 'Victory Over Japan', and 'The Unconquerable Soul' (which displayed the spirit of the Czechoslovakian, Russian and Polish people during the war). They also ranged considerably in size.

'London Pride' for example, was entirely photographic, the pictures giving expression to the wonderful spirit of London during the blitzkrieg. A complete cross-section of London life was shown, from the fire watcher down to the shelterer, and from the King and Queen to the humblest resident of Stepney. The photographs were selected from large numbers of agencies and studios and their enlargement gave them particular intensity. The presentation of these pictures was the work of Milner Gray who showed a rare skill and understanding in his choice. The exhibition, in fact, established a lead in the field.

In contrast to trade fairs and national and international exhibitions before the war, the MoI exhibitions, due to the circumstances of the war, explored various persuasive techniques geared to attitude rather than sales. Most of the

Display from 'London Pride', the first exhibition designed by Milner Gray as Head of the exhibitions branch in 1940.

exhibitions had virtually nothing to show in terms of exhibitable objects, but they still managed to hold the audience's attention. As Misha Black later wrote:

'Exceptional circumstances exist, however, when the subject matter is of such intrinsic interest that large numbers of the public have a passionate desire to obtain information about it . . . This was true about some of the wartime exhibitions when many thousands of people patiently studied comparatively long captions explaining how civilians should deal with poison gas or fire bombs, or how most efficiently to rear pigs and rabbits in the back yard.'[23]

As Julian Trevelyan noted in his autobiography,

'. . . the public was hungry for pictures'.[24]

'London Pride', as has been said was the first exhibition produced by the MoI. Initially it was conceived and designed by Milner Gray working alone before he had recruited any staff. It was held at Charing Cross underground station and dealt with the civilian effort of the Londoners.

The dramatic 'Poison Gas' exhibition, which was held on the same site in 1941, was of a similar format but more instructional in content. The exhibition was designed by the staff of the exhibitions division assisted by F. H. K. Henrion who commissioned many of the photographs and also designed the photographic poster which seemed to startle people into

Entrance hall for the 'America Marches' exhibition in 1942.

'Soviet at War' poster. Designed by Gray in 1943.

visiting the exhibition. Again the display techniques hinged round the use of photographic plaques and photomontages, but a greater emphasis on 3D displays illustrated the advances the exhibition team had made. Picture diagrams of cut-out figures recounted the story of poison gas and the importance of using gas masks. An exhibition unit threading through the centre of the site showed the 'Birth of the Gas Mask' with the object displayed at different stages of its development. At the end of the display the visitor was urged to have his respirator tested immediately in the van outside the station.

Humour, however, was not lacking and could be found in the 'Bread into Battle' exhibition at

Charing Cross; the 'Out Rats' outdoor exhibition, with displays such as 'Routing the Rats' and a carefully stylised approach warning of the dangers of rats; and in the 'Private Scrap Builds a Bomber', advising on economies. The 'Dig for Victory' exhibition also adopted a humorous approach.

Most of the small and medium-sized exhibitions, such as the 'Life-Line', 'Free Europe's Forces', 'The March of a Nation', 'New Life to the Land', and 'Fuel Transport' exhibitions demanded that a story be told. The exhibitions were then developed according to a script in a narrative form. A variety of copywriters with advertising or journalistic backgrounds were used by the branch to collaborate with the graphic designers in preparation of the exhibition scripts. George Orwell wrote the text for 'Free Europe's Forces'. Robert Sinclair, who was Features Editor of *The Star*, wrote the words for 'Poison Gas', 'How to Fight the Fire Bomb' and 'America Marches'. A. L. Lloyd wrote the story for the 'Life-Line' exhibition which dealt with the work of the Navy in wartime. The texts were obviously prepared in close liaison with the sponsoring government departments and with the copy column of the exhibitions branch which included Alan Martin Harvey, G. Tringham, G. Bussey and D. Phillips, none of whom were trained specialists but, in essence, 'jobbing copywriters'.

The poster publicity designed for the exhibitions was usually produced by the individuals involved on particular exhibitions, whether they were on the permanent staff or designing freelance. A regular contract also existed between the exhibitions division and Dorlands Advertising Agency for the handling of the MoI exhibition advertising. Posters, press advertisements and coloured demi-octavo leaflets and window stickers were produced in conjunction with each exhibition rather than catalogues, because paper shortages kept publicity to a minimum.

A great variety of exhibition sites were used by the MoI. Charing Cross underground station was usually used as a site for launching exhibitions: Ministers often went there to open a display and to make a speech. 'Gangway Please', 'Fireguard', 'Fighting Fit', 'Private Scrap Goes to the Front', 'Our Eastern Job', 'China at War' and the 'Firewatchers' exhibitions were all held there. The Regents Park Zoo was the site for the 'Off the Ration' exhibition in 1943. This was designed by Milner Gray with Bronek Katz and F. H. K. Henrion, with illustrations by Lewitt-Him. This exhibition described different ways of keeping pets economically in wartime and explained what could be used as food. The covered outside walk, with canvas zig-zag lashed between tubular steel frames, added to the accessible, friendly atmosphere at this exhibition. The approach was light-hearted and the text was easy reading and less didactic than some of the others. To echo the rope lashing, new rope lettering designed by Monotype in 1938 was used in the plaques and posters. Tall stilt-like see-through wooden structures circumscribed the area. This was particularly aimed at children and animal lovers, and it was well received.

'The Army' exhibition of 1943 was held on the bomb site of the John Lewis store in Oxford Street. This was one of the most popular of all the MoI exhibitions, the site itself being ready made with both open and enclosed areas, silhouetted walls and enclosed passages. The AIA had used this site earlier that year for their exhibition of paintings 'For Liberty'. The Royal Engineers added to its suitability by constructing both underground trenches and a temporary overhead bridge which visitors were obliged to cross. This exhibition covered 56 000 square feet and showed 23 000 exhibits. Huge queues waited to see the detailed information placed before them.

Although this exhibition required great organisation and security, it was nevertheless less of a display problem than some of the more abstract exhibitions already dealt with by the division. All the same great ingenuity was called into play in arranging so many objects. The Dorland Hall, off Lower Regent Street, was also used by the MoI once or twice for exhibitions such as 'America Marches' and 'Save Fuel'.

The policies of the exhibitions branch during its first two years of activity were fairly broad, accommodating the general requirement of government publicity as the needs arose. By 1943, however, exhibition ideas were more closely formulated with a very positive aim, to

The 'Trap the germs in your handkerchief' exhibition.

promote national reconstruction in a moral and material sense. 'To form and educate public opinion as to the requirements of social reconstruction in production, finance, social effort and unity by demonstrating the efficient planning for reconstruction of a new Britain.'[25] The ideas of what England had stood for in the past — the notions of liberty and democracy — were consequently emphasised strongly.

A major break from the early stage in the exhibitions division was made when Clifford Bloxham was appointed administrative head of the division in November 1941, moving from his post as Deputy Director-General of the general production division. He had been advertising manager for John Lewis store from 1923 to 1929 and this change-over in the division was apparently due to its developing size. Milner Gray remained, however, as Head of the creative section of the division and was given the title of Principal Design Adviser. Bloxham altered the situation radically, aimed for the doubling of his staff and drew up a vast scheme for re-organising the MoI's display and exhibition work.[26]

Public reaction to these MoI exhibitions is now difficult to assess. The attendance figures are very favourable and photographs often show tremendous queues waiting to see the displays. Three and a half million people visited the 'Army' exhibition in London during its tour of Britain and one and a half million attended the 'Victory over Japan' exhibition (1945). The MoI kept attendance figures where this was practicable; for instance, 561 164 people were attracted to the 'Off the Ration' exhibition which ran for 61 days at Regents Park and the 'Nazi Way of Life' exhibition held in Doncaster in 1943 was visited during its eight days by 54 000 – though the population of the town was only 72 000 at this time. A counting device installed at the Charing Cross underground exhibition site recorded some interesting, if erratic, attendance figures. Some 66 252 people saw the 'America Marches' exhibition during its 25 day stretch and it was estimated that out of the 270 days on which the underground site was occupied during the year 1942–3, an average of 3934 people visited an exhibition daily. However, since it was apparently possible to enter the display area without being registered by the electronic eye, these official figures should be treated as a conservative estimate of attendance numbers.

Contemporary design magazines, such as the *Architectural Review* and *Art and Industry*, praised the MoI results: 'Top marks for a Government department' said the *Architectural Review*.[27] *Art and Industry* gave much precious space for consideration of '. . . the dramatic principle in exhibition technique' and '. . . the excellent marshalling of incidents and their portrayal by means of large panel drawings'[28] as these were exploited in the 'Unconquerable Soul' exhibition.

The few exhibitions which were staged by bodies other than the MoI during the war tended to enhance the progressive feature of the Government work but, on the whole, exhibition design during the Second World War was sharply divided into the two sections: Ministry of Information exhibitions and non-Ministry exhibitions. Writing in 1946, Peter Austen described the history of the British war-time exhibition as that of: '. . . gallant enterprise in adverse circumstances'.[29]

With greater hindsight, the circumstances, albeit tumultuous, seem to have been more hospitable to the designers than the preceding peace. Not only in the field of exhibition design, but in other fields also, such as poster design and camouflage. Fiona MacCarthy has pointed out:

Rendering of the Royal Coat of Arms for incised and colour-filled wood panels for use on Ministry of Information exhibitions. Designed by Gray in 1941.

'Wartime, for designers, was a kind of golden age in which almost unlimited money and labour were forthcoming to pursue the wildest fancies, masterpieces of inventiveness.'[30]

Whilst this may be slightly exaggerated, the designers themselves recalled the period with great fondness as a very happy working time, where competition was on an entirely amicable basis. The pre-war freelance designer, whether employed full-time or occasionally, by the MoI, undoubtedly benefited from the establishment of this official publicity organisation and many reputations were made in the design field during the Second World War.

When Milner Gray left the MoI, the staff of the creative section presented him with a silver-gilt and enamel bowl inscribed: 'From MoI.DE2 to Milner Gray, who created a design team to which it has been a privilege to belong.'

Design Research Unit

Apart from his work for the ministry, described in the previous chapter, Milner Gray also spent time during the war in keeping the SIAD alive and with laying the foundations for a new design group practice which, he hoped, could be set up when the war was over.

James Holland has written of these years:

'A period of widespread confusion followed the declaration of war. Large-scale evacuation helped to create this, with some colleges and schools not reopening in the autumn, and some studios and units closing down for lack of commissions or prospects. Artists, architects, designers and others who earlier had fled from central Europe, and in many cases had settled themselves successfully into the native environment, were rounded up and hustled off to internment on the Isle of Man.

'Fortunately in most cases this detention did not last for long and some designers had the experience of being behind the wire one week and being commissioned on official projects the next. It was not only designers from Europe who found themselves in a situation of such uncertainty. Industrial production would need to be re-aligned to war production, advertising would diminish and disappear, materials and resources be diverted from the commercial market. There would certainly be some work for a few designers – recruiting posters updated, morale-sustaining publications, camouflage. During the months of the so-called phoney war, it was not even easy to join the armed forces. Eventually a new pattern of existence was to impose itself, and though the opportunities for design employment were limited, they were not negligible . . .'[31]

They included the utility ranges of furniture and clothing, planned under the direction of Gordon Russell, a Fellow of the Society of Industrial Artists; and various re-housing projects from pre-fabs to more permanent schemes for local authorities.

Peter Ray wrote of this time:

'In London the chance grouping of the Ministry of Information Exhibition designers led to musing on the post-war future of the profession. A London group was formed under the chairmanship of Milner Gray with Peter Ray as Honorary Secretary to turn the musing into positive discussion.

'The Group met weekly in cafes and restaurants in Marchmont Street and Charlotte Street . . . and gradually formulated a scheme for the rebirth of the society on a new professional basis instead of the previous craft-based entry. The plan called for the resignation or cancellation of all the existing membership and re-application with acceptance of a new Code of Conduct. Design practice would be for more mass, or at least batch, production, and acceptance would depend on submission of work of an acceptable standard. The final plan was put to an extraordinary meeting held in the Council Chamber of the Royal Institute of British Architects. Getting together a quorum for the meeting was a major headache, particularly as we were anxious to recruit industrial designers.

Our support came from Wells Coates, Frederick Gibberd, Keith Murray and Brian O'Rorke. For graphics, Henrion and Ashley Havinden gave a lot of time, the latter with his wife, Margaret, giving us meeting room and secretarial support at Crawfords for a lengthy period. We also had meeting facilities at the National Gallery during 1944 and 1945. The SIAD London group consisted of Milner Gray, Misha Black, Peter Ray, Ron Dickens and F. E. Middleditch.'

Milner Gray, President of the SIA from 1943 to 1948, also acted as Chairman of the Drafting

Committee for an SIA Memorandum to the Board of Education on 'The Training of Designers for Industry'.

Birth of DRU

Although, at this time, the bombing of Britain was at its height, the very destruction indicated that, if Britain survived the war at all, one of the urgent needs would be to supply industry with new designs to replace those which had been manufactured prior to 1939.

This need was foreseen not only by designers but also by people in the grimly restricted advertising business, and Marcus Brumwell (then Chairman and Managing Director of Stuarts' advertising agency) decided to do something about it. He invited his friend Herbert Read, the distinguished design historian, critic and author of *Art and Industry*, to a ration-restricted dinner at his house in Surrey to formulate the first ideas for a group of designers and artists.

Brumwell and Read then discussed these proposals with Cecil D. Notley who was then head of Notley Advertising and was another member of the Advertising Service Guild. As a result of these discussions, Notley turned to Milner Gray whom he invited to set down on paper a detailed plan for the kind of design service they felt would be needed. Gray, who was already planning for the renewal of his pre-war practice, sent his ideas to Notley and the plan he put forward laid the foundations of IDP's successor, Design Research Unit, on 1 January 1943.

Gray wrote to Notley,

'The purpose of the formation of a group such as is envisaged is to make available immediately a design service equipped to advise on all problems of design, and to form a nucleus group which, through contacts established during the war period with specialist designers and experts in all appropriate fields, would be in a position at the end of the war to expand and to undertake the wider services which may then be demanded of it. The final aim is to present a service so complete that it could undertake any design case which might confront the State, Municipal Authorities, Industry or Commerce'.

He went on to describe the organisation of his proposed design group in some detail.

His suggestions were accepted, and Herbert Read, DRU's first manager and, for the time being, sole member of staff, installed himself in a small office in Kingsway from which he set out to introduce to potential clients the new service the unit offered.

In many ways Read was the most unlikely of individuals to find himself in charge of an operation intended to convince a highly sceptical industry that a new-fangled activity called industrial design had any relevance to its interests. A poet, literary critic, philosopher and acknowledged authority on design, he was the gentlest of men, with a manner so shy and quiet that when he spoke it was often difficult to hear what he said. But he knew most of the leading artists and designers and was liked and respected by them.

The contacts with industry, on the other hand, were known to Marcus Brumwell, Cecil Notley and other members of the Advertising Service Guild, including Everett Jones and Rupert Casson.

Their task was to bring the two sides together, to create a nucleus of designers and to persuade industry to employ them. With this in mind, Read co-opted DRU's first team of associates, which included Gray and Black, the architects Frederick Gibberd and Sadie Speight, the structural engineer Felix Samuely and the designer Norbert Dutton, all of whom continued to run their own practices, except for Black, Gray and

Dutton who were then still employed at the Ministry of Information.

The unit got under way but, by the end of the first year, publicising the service and organising the few commissions that were received required more time than Herbert Read was able to give. Therefore, early in 1944, DRU advertised for a full-time manager. Among those applied was Bernard Hollowood, an economist by training, who was then a teacher at Loughborough College and subsequently became widely known as editor of *Punch*. He had been deeply interested in design, less from an idealistic point of view than from the standpoint of an economist who was well aware of how important design would become after the war if Britain was to achieve the 75 per cent increase in the volume of exports which Sir Stafford Cripps had announced would be essential. He got the job, but stayed for only three months as he was then offered the assistant editorship of *The Economist*.

Hollowood has recalled his excitement at the prospect of working with Herbert Read, whom he had admired from his writing but had not met. 'It was like God descending,' he said, 'it was always an effort for him to become a man of the world and, although he had other business interests, he always longed to be back in the peaceful surroundings of his Yorkshire home.'

Bernard Hollowood's work, when he went to *The Economist*, was taken over by Bill Vaugham, who had been a colleague of Gray's at the Ministry, and who stayed on with DRU until 1946, when the founder partners were released from their wartime jobs and the unit came to life as a more fully active organisation.

In 1944–45, Gray designed an exhibition entitled 'Design at Home', which was organised by the Council for the Encouragement of Music and the Arts (later the Arts Council) and held at the National Gallery with the permission of Kenneth Clark, the Director. This exhibition opened on VE Day, 8 May 1945, and contained

One of the sections from the 'Design at Home' exhibition at the National Gallery in 1945. Designed for the CEMA by Gray in collaboration with Kenneth Bayes and Peter Ray.

examples of utility furniture in room settings which firmly established the new concern for a sense of order, with carefully aligned surfaces and an airy spaciousness in keeping with the then current ideals. Gray has recalled that, on one occasion when they were planning the exhibition during a heavy air raid, he, Kenneth Clark and Sam Courtauld had to continue their discussion under their conference table. Judith Ann Freeman wrote, about this exhibition:

'CEMA took a first step in the design propaganda direction by stating the "Design at Home" exhibition at the National Gallery in 1945. The aim was to guide the public in the furnishing and decoration of their homes, for the end of the war would herald widespread rehousing. The emphasis was on individuality within mass production, with the slogan: "Make the home human in a way that is both personal and creative." That is the message with which visitors will leave the exhibition. "You are the designer of your home."

'Furnishings and furniture were the main exhibits arranged within individual room-settings such as a "family sitting room" and a "bachelor bed-sitting room". The chief designer and organiser was Milner Gray; Noel Carrington wrote the introduction to the brochure and Kenneth Bayes, F. H. K. Henrion, Bronek Katz and Peter Ray assisted, with the Board of Trade acting as advisors. Though small in scale, the object and approach of the exhibition were elaborated upon the following year by the newly-formed Council of Industrial Design.'[32]

Exhibits included 'Radaware' cast iron cooking utensils by Radiation Ltd; a hammock-principle long-back easy chair manufactured by Christie-Tyler and designed by Milner Gray; a 'Kyrnric' cotton tufted washable rug designed by Sadie Speight; a silver tobacco jar designed by A. E.

Harvey and made by Hukin and Heath; a low tea table in natural waxed oak made by Gordon Russell Ltd; Bernard Leach pottery; Denby pottery; a wash basin made from Perspex sheet, designed by Milner Gray and made by ICI; a tea service made by Foley China and designed by Graham Sutherland; 'Garden' pattern dinnerware by Eric Ravilious; and wooden toys by Paul and Marjorie Abbatt Ltd.

Other work

The Council of Industrial Design was set up in December 1944, and was to be a major spur to a generation of designers and architects. A report called *The Visual Arts*, prepared by Political and Economic Planning in 1946, emphasised that, since '. . . every effort to improve design in the past has failed for lack of continuity, it is to be hoped that the new Council will receive adequate support over the period of years which it must take to establish itself.'

One of the first important activities of the Council was to provide a public stimulus in the form of a major national exhibition of industrial design called 'Britain Can Make It'. Its brief included an explanation of what was involved in the design process and the need in industry for the special skills which the industrial designer could provide. This part of the exhibition was given to Design Research Unit and Milner Gray led the team of graphic designers.

The exhibition display, however, was designed by Misha Black and, using an egg-cup as an example, he explained how even the simplest mass-produced product creates a multitude of problems which it is the designer's job to solve. To prove the point, a display of some 60 different egg-cups illustrated the large area of freedom still left to the designer. It was a highly educational approach and continued the pattern for narrative displays which had been begun by Milner Gray in the MoI and has been characteristic of British exhibitions ever since. It also revealed a British fondness for coating educational pills with whimsy which today seems distinctly over-sweet but at the time was understood by and delighted the crowds who queued – nearly half a million strong during the whole run of the exhibition – to shuffle through the rooms of the Victoria and Albert Museum.

For the majority of these visitors, however, the products shown elsewhere in the exhibition would merely whet their appetite, for the pleasure of buying was largely to be denied them. Decorated china, sumptuous kitchens and new domestic products of all kinds were to remain in short supply for another four or five years, most of them being destined for 'export only'.

Milner Gray exhibited projects for an improved taxi-cab and cooker. The cab incorporated amongst other improvements a new device – an illuminated roof indicator soon to be adopted by all London taxicabs.

Research

The description of the industrial design process given in the egg-cup exhibit was part of a much wider interest at that time in explaining the function of the new activity of industrial design to an industry which at best was unfamiliar with it and possibly willing to learn, but otherwise was highly sceptical. In 1946, DRU's partners and associates, including Black, Dutton, Gray, Gibberd, Martin, Speight and Samuely, together with others not connected to the unit, contributed individual chapters to a book on *The Practice of Design*[33] for which Herbert Read wrote an introduction. A small booklet produced by DRU about the same time, *Industrial Design*, and circulated widely to industry, summed up the main theme of the larger book in more general terms.

To some extent the ideas which it expressed seemed hardly to have changed since before the war. It said, for example, that 'Industrial design is the intelligent, practical and skilled association of art with industry.' And, later, in describing the qualities that the industrial designer could bring to the service of industry:

'First and foremost the industrial designer is a fully qualified technician. He (or she) may be an architect, a scientist, an engineer, a fellow of the Society of Industrial Artists, but whatever the technicalities of his training he is basically an artist – one who has trained to know good proportions, clean lines, well blended or contrasted colours, and who can demonstrate this on paper with brush and pigment.'

However, it went on to emphasise the practical skills which the industrial designer could provide and the section on design research is particularly significant in explaining the seriousness of purpose which DRU wanted to put forward as the special quality of post-war design services. 'Successful design,' it said, 'is based on data, not on inspiration alone . . . What is the existing or potential market, its extent and type? What competition exists? What are the comparative advantages of the principal competitive product? What possible advantages have not been developed? What are the opportunities for enlarging and developing the market to other fields?'

That research is an essential preliminary to design was a refrain which was repeated at every opportunity in the early years. IDP had found it an essential, and emphasis of this part of DRU's service was certainly needed to dispel the popular idea at the time that industrial design was the last-minute 'tarting up' of a product of which the essential form had already been settled. The ability to express this need in convincing terms rapidly developed in the years which followed. In a paper to the Royal Society of Arts in 1949, Milner Gray expanded on this philosophy in terms which are relevant today:

'In Great Britain during the second world war the production of armaments and essential goods imposed on industry necessary economies in skill, time, material and effort. In certain fields, such as the development of aircraft production, and the technique of packing warlike stores, to quote only two examples, the encouragement of design closely integrated with production became a sheer necessity for survival. And so in the 1960s the attitude of the more informed propagandist for the better design of machine-made goods has developed a bias towards the needs of production. Design for *selling* has given way to design for *making*. From the cosy gatherings of the converted and the high ideals of the highbrows of the 1920s, industrial design comes down to earth.'

It was design for production, he went on to say, which brought into focus the new need for detailed planning and research. 'The separation of the manufacturer from his market, implicit in a highly mechanised society, compels him to re-establish contact with it through market research . . . You cannot make 100000 copies of an article which nobody wants – at least you are not likely to be asked to do so more than once.'

However, fact-finding was not the only reason he gave for research. Facts about production equipment and methods, and about distribution and handling, were all essential preliminaries to design, for only after all the information had been properly assembled, analysed and digested could the design work itself begin. 'But in the long run,' Gray concluded, 'it is his aesthetic faculty which differentiates the designer from the mere technician.'

Although it had been the intention of DRU at the beginning to offer a complete service of research and design, the idea was found to be too ambitious. How could any design organisation hope to encompass research in depth for all the materials and technologies, the production methods and markets, and for all the industries which it would encounter in the course of its work? For one thing, industry was not prepared to pay for this amount of work; for another, new research organisations, both private and state supported, were beginning to be set up which were far more capable than a design office of carrying out the types of research that were required. At the same time DRU found itself with more design work than it could easily do. So, at least in areas such as its export research organisation, which had been rather optimistically set up in 1946, DRU's intention to establish research services soon became modified by practicality.

DRU organisation

Until this time, DRU had been working in cramped conditions, huddled into three rooms in Bedford Square. 'In one large room,' Dorothy Goslett remembers, 'there were Misha, Milner, myself, Austin Frazer, Jo Revill, the plan chest, the boardroom table and almost everything else, and one telephone between the lot of us.' Dorothy Goslett, who was a campaigns officer in the exhibitions division with Milner Gray and Misha Black at the Ministry of Information during the war, became, in peace time, DRU's business manager.

To run DRU efficiently, re-organisation was clearly needed and this became possible when Marcus Brumwell bought up all the shares from the Advertising Services Guild and became the unit's majority shareholder, establishing a holding company with Misha Black and Milner Gray to control its finances. This change made for a much tighter direction of financial policy and DRU moved again, this time to its own offices in Park Street.

JEAN STRAKER

Model and drawings for an improved taxicab, commissioned by the Council of Industrial Design for showing at the 'Britain Can Make It' exhibition in 1946. This design introduced the roof light indicator, promptly adopted by all London taxicabs. Other proposed improvements included the positioning of the engine to one side of the driver's seat; direct and relayed communication between passenger and driver; sliding doors; and a single cushioned front seat which could be inverted to accommodate light luggage. Designed by Gray with William Vaughan and George Williams.

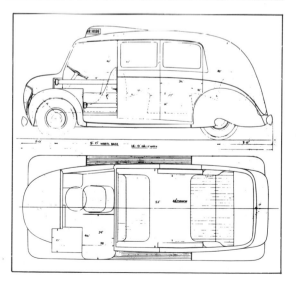

A new form of associateship was introduced, for a group of designers who, after war service, wanted to set up in practice for themselves but had insufficient capital to do so. DRU offered them office space, services, and a financial pool from which they could draw each month an agreed sum, which was later set off against their total earnings. In return, the associates gave priority to DRU work, over and above their other commissions. Their final income from the unit was worked out on the basis of an agreed proportion of the fees for each job; a system which left them, at the end of each year, either with a lump sum due to them or, more rarely, with a deficit to be cleared. Such a system worked well for DRU because it enabled them to use designers of a higher calibre than they could have afforded to employ on a full-time basis. It also suited the associates because it provided them with a base for their operations, a degree of financial security and sufficient freedom to enable them to build up their own practices.

The structure of the office at this time thus consisted of Brumwell, the financial controller, who delegated executive responsibility to a partner of Stuart Advertising, H. C. Timewell; Read, director; three founder partners, Gray, Black and Bayes; the business manager, Goslett; several associate members, who included Robert Gutmann and Ronald Ingles; and, increasingly, a number of younger salaried designers and architects including John Diamond, Clifford Hatts, Herbert Spencer and George Williams.

The unit was organised on strictly democratic lines. Gray and Black brought in most of the work through their personal reputations, but they did not act as 'bosses' who handed out the work and told other people what to do. It was essentially a group operation among friends in which each job was discussed among everyone

concerned and the work was carried out by whoever was thought best qualified to tackle it, a link back to the co-operative structure of the Bassett-Gray and IDP forerunners. To maintain this sense of shared purpose and democratic exchange of ideas, a regular six-weekly discussion meeting among all design staff and some clerical personnel was established and remained sacrosanct as an institution throughout the entire history of DRU. At these meetings work on current jobs was presented and explained by the designers concerned and everybody had an opportunity to comment or criticise. Although they were informal, the meetings were conducted by a chairman – one of the partners – and were usually attended by Sir Herbert Read, until his death. A guest critic was sometimes invited, someone from industry or the trade press, partly to introduce an objective view from outside the unit and partly to give the meetings a secondary use as a public relations exercise.

Perhaps more important to the work of the office than either of these purposes was the educational aspect of the discussions for everybody involved. Few punches were pulled when work was criticised and designers soon became skilled in defending their work on a logical basis. The younger designers, particularly, were encouraged to take part in the discussions, not only as part of their own training but also to teach, since the senior partners frankly admitted that they looked to the younger members of the unit to keep the rest aware of new attitudes and ideas.

Exhibition work and other activities

DRU expanded rapidly during the late 1940s but, in spite of the emphasis on product design in such work as the egg-cup exhibit at 'Britain Can Make it', comparatively few commissions for product design work came into the office. What did seem to impress potential clients who saw

DRU Design Directorate at a meeting in 1948.

'Design at Work' exhibition at Burlington House in October 1948. The exhibition was to show the work of the Royal Designers for Industry. It was designed and produced by DRU for the Royal Society of Arts and the Council of Industrial Design.

Needle wrappers marketed under the name of Milwards by Needle Industries Ltd.

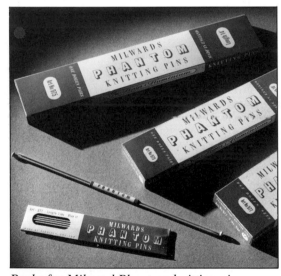

Packs for Milward Phantom knitting pins designed by Gray in 1947. The range formed a sub-division of a wide range of knitting pins and needles marketed under the name of Milwards for which a generic style was established with modifications to differentiate the various categories of products in the range. The cartons and wrappers in the division shown were printed in one colour — a light venetian red on an off-white board.

the exhibition was the skill with which it had been designed. This led to further commissions for exhibitions, including 'Darkness into Daylight', a display of lighting equipment sponsored by the Electric Lamp Manufacturers' Association; 'Design at Work', an exhibition at the Royal Academy, organised by the CoID and the Royal Society of Arts, of work by members of the Faculty of Royal Designers for Industry; and a growing number of stands at trade shows such as the British Industries Fair.

'Design at Work' was planned and co-ordinated by Milner Gray and included examples of his own work as an RDI, notably his corporate design for Ilford as well as packaging for Milwards range of knitting pins and needles.

The President of the Board of Trade, Harold Wilson, wrote about the exhibition in the *Board of Trade Journal* of October 1948:

'In less than three years from now, during the 1951 Festival of Britain, we hope that the cream of Britain's industrial production will be on display for the critical scrutiny of visitors from all over the world. We must not show them goods that fall below the highest possible level of design.

'Many of our visitors will be coming from overseas markets with growing local industries of their own; many more will come from countries as highly industrialised as our own. They will look to us not for goods of ordinary quality and design but for something outstanding. Only goods which work well, look well and sell well will win the export battle . . .

'I urge manufacturers to mark the lessons of this exhibition "Design at Work", to make it a specific function of management to bring the designer into his right place in the industrial organisation; to give him the status that will enable him to co-operate as an equal with the production engineers on the one hand and the

Original sketch designs for the interior treatment of the Bristol Wayfarer by Gray. Misha Black was also associated with this project.

sales staffs on the other. This is something that needs attention from the top — and it will surely pay handsomely.

'I congratulate the Council of Industrial Design and the Royal Society of Arts, both of whom have responsibilities in connection with the 1951 Festival, for staging this important and timely forerunner. I am glad, also, that we shall have this opportunity of seeing for the first time under one roof the work of the Royal Designers for Industry.'

All the messages contained in this speech became the burden of a lecture tour Gray made

in 1949. He not only delivered a series of lecture on Industrial Design, dealing with design standards and developments in Great Britain, he also held consultations on the organisation and training of designers with designers' associations, government officials and educational authorities.

From 1947 to 1952, he became a member of the Ministry of Education Advisory Committee on Art Examinations. Again in 1947 he was commissioned to design a new Ascot Gold Cup won by M. Bussac, the French industrialist.

From 1947 to 1950, Gray was design consul-

Design for the 1947 Ascot Gold Cup by Gray. The cup was supplied through the Royal Warrant holders, D & J Welby Ltd, made by W. E. King and engraved by G. T. Friend.

tant to D & J Welby Ltd for silver and metal-ware. He also designed a range of heavy gauge aluminium hollow-ware for the Midland Metal Spinning Company.

House style extended to 'Corporate Identity'

Perhaps Milner Gray's most important work at this period was in the field of 'house style', later called 'corporate identity'. Two schemes begun in 1946 were for a revised symbol, house style and package designs for the Rolex watch company and a scheme for offices, showrooms, exhibitions and packaging for Ilford Ltd. These schemes were carried out over several years.

The idea that design could be used as a business tool, to express a firm's unique identity through all aspects of its operation, had existed in theory before the war, but its realisation was very much a post-war phenomenon and developed on a large scale only during these ten or fifteen years.

Writing in the Swiss publication *Emballages* in 1949, Gray said:

Tankards designed by Gray for D & J Welby Ltd in 1947–8.

Frypan and milk saucepan for the Midland Metal Spinners Company.

Acrylic watch case designed by Gray in 1946 as part of a packaging range for the Rolex watch company's 'Oyster' waterproof watch.

'. . . a corporate identity programme implies the co-ordination of every aspect of a company's business which may have a visual impact on the public, so that everything associated with the firm, from the appearance of the commodities they manufacture to that of the packages which protect them, the trucks in which they are delivered or the publicity material which advertises them is identified with the source of its origin.'

Again in 1959, DRU reported on the Ilford Corporate Identity Scheme:

'The simplicity of the surface treatment and the bold and colourful interpretation of the name ILFORD effectively ensured that the impact of a small unit such as this on the potential customer is emphatic when seen either singly or in a mass display. The film categories are differentiated by a marked colour change of the cartons, the majority of the packings being printed in two colours on yellow tinted stock and varnished. Essential coding, size, category and speed are accommodated on the carton ends, making for easy recognition on the dealer's shelves.

'The Ilford transport fleet employs the company's house colours of chrome yellow counterchanged with flame red and the condensed sans-serif letter-forms which are

Oxford Street Shop front for Ilford Ltd, 1946.

associated throughout with the company's name and presentation material. A Royal Coat of Arms is in full colour and the lettering in white and black.'

This was DRU's first involvement in a comprehensive design programme and it established a relationship which continued afterwards and was the beginning of several long-term consultancies for which Milner Gray led the team. In this way, the Unit's graphic designers provided advice on the visual implications of such things as trade-marks, stationery, packaging, catalogues, signposting, vehicle liveries and uniforms as part of a joint team with the unit's architects, interior and product designers, who were brought in as necessary to deal with the design of shops, showrooms, offices, factory layouts and products. Projects of this kind were carried out for Courage and for Watneys, the brewery companies; Gilbey's the wine merchants; the Hodder Group of publishing companies; Dunlop; Capper Neil, the building contractors; the multi-product company Thomas de la Rue; and, later, British Rail, ICI and others.

In the early post-war years such schemes were referred to as 'house styles'. The description seemed appropriate because it referred to the establishment of a recognisable visual image for an individual firm. The structure of industry, however, began to change rapidly during the 1960s when companies amalgamated in ever more complex patterns of organisation. In such conditions the term 'house style' no longer fitted the new problem of creating a common identity out of a conglomerate association of different firms, each with its own character and methods of work. What was often needed was a 'corporate identity', and this term, borrowed from America where the restructuring of industry had begun some years earlier, was now widely adopted in Britain.

From the designer's point of view, the difference between a 'house style' and a 'corporate identity programme' was only one of scale. This was reflected less in the amount of design work which had to be done than in the problems of management and organisation. Few large companies appreciate at first the implications of a decision to go ahead with a corporate identity programme. To most of them, it is considered as a cosmetic operation, with the creation of a more attractive image by surface decoration.

What they overlook is that no amount of make-up can rejuvenate an ageing face. Corporate identity programmes have therefore to focus attention on more fundamental aspects of business health, and this was seen by DRU to be directly in line with the wider concern in industry with the efficiency of its management. There was little point in having a letterheading that evoked an impression of an efficient, forward-looking company if the letter written on it was badly typed, rude, or illiterate. Nor was there any value in a luxurious-looking pack for a poor quality product.

While these might seem to be comparatively minor issues in themselves, they emphasised the need for a corporate attitude throughout the management hierarchy of a company. They also affected more important questions which were central to management policy. A group of companies could well find that corporate identity was in conflict with its policy of competition among its subsidiaries. In these circumstances a *corporate* identity might not be required at all, and design programmes of a different kind would be needed.

Therefore, for DRU, work on such programmes was found to extend far beyond the graphic orientation of most corporate identity programmes into the design of many other aspects of the company's activities. The term 'corporate design' was then used to express the nature of such extensive design programmes and several examples of these, by DRU, are illustrated in this book.

Once again, therefore, Milner Gray was ahead of the need in evolving a pattern of investigation which was of value when carrying out corporate design programmes for some of the largest industrial organisations in Britain. Both Gray and Black believed that it was essential that initial discussions should take place at a top management level, so that the major policy issues could be resolved at the start. From such discussions, a series of questions for management could be formulated which the company might be asked to think about so that the brief could be set out in broad principle. Since the subsidiaries and associated companies of large organisations often have a considerable degree of autonomy, there could be no military chain of command enabling orders issued at the top to be carried out unquestioningly by those below. It was therefore necessary to set up a committee or

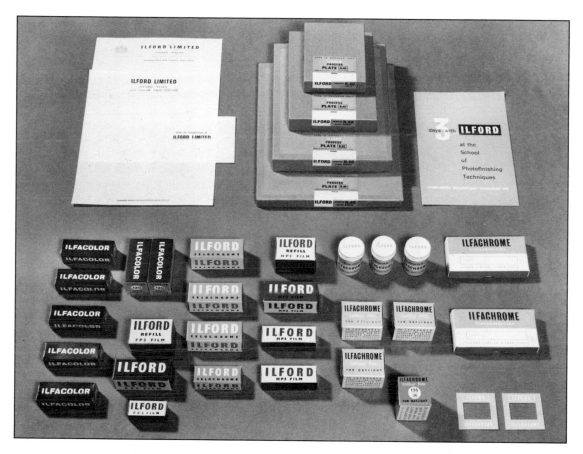

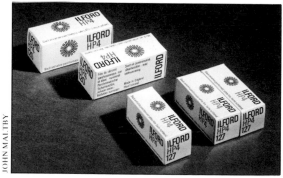

Range of cartons, stationery and printed matter showing how the house style was applied to this part of Ilford's activities.

Ilford film cartons for the second phase of the corporate identity scheme in 1966.

JOHN MALTBY

Ilford stand at the International Printing exhibition, Olympia, in 1955. Designed by Milner Gray and Robert Gutman during phase 1 of the scheme.

working party in which representatives of the associated companies could participate in a mutually agreed plan. These committees had two main functions: the first was to examine and, if necessary, reinforce the need for corporate action; and the second to provide a 'communications channel' through which information could be collected and reactions to initial design solutions tested.

Having set up the administrative machinery, the next stage was an on-the-spot investigation by members of the design team, preferably accompanied by the client's own representatives. Such fact-finding surveys could be exten-

sive. The accumulated information from these investigations, and from discussions with the client, was analysed and the results set out in a report which defined the problem and proposed appropriate solutions and working procedures. These reports, which for a job of major complexity might well be in the region of 30000 words long, were intended more to record an agreed stage in the progress of the work than to present the client with totally unexpected proposals. They therefore provided the basis for a detailed understanding between client and designer from which design work itself could proceed through all its stages.

Gray, for his own part, built up a checklist of some 150 questions to put to clients before a corporate identity programme began and was known to work patiently through all of these in order to establish his client's precise requirements. To use such a checklist had many virtues, for it meant that companies were forced to think about problems which they had not previously considered. What might have started as a simple commission to redesign a firm's stationery could be shown to be only part of the problem, and sometimes not the most important part.

The corporate identity programme for Austin Reed Ltd included a new trade symbol, a characteristic letterform for the company's name, with a secondary letter for subsidiary descriptions, the adoption of a basic house colour with complementary variants, and the use of a selected number of patterns for packaging and display. These formed the basis of a scheme which established an easily recognised style for the company and its retail shops, goods and services.[34]

From 1949 to 1955, Gray acted as design consultant to Courage and Company for a corporate identity scheme, this time including a public house identification programme. About this, Reyner Banham recorded:

ALFRED CRACKNELL

Packaging and stationery for Austin Reed Ltd.
designed by Gray and Kenneth Lamble and
incorporating the trade mark which Gray
designed.

'The new Courage typeface makes an intelligent compromise between the elegance of Eric Gill's Perpetua which the letter forms resemble somewhat and the blunt, no-nonsense quality of the traditional Egyptians and the way in which it is employed by Milner Gray on the tray is a salutory demonstration of the art of being decorative without using decoration. Not even the two little stars are purely decorative, since they serve as punctuation between two slogans. The cockerel has a real and important function as a trademark, and the function of the slogans is obvious, but no-one can say that this is an example of that 'spiritual barren-ness' that is supposed to be a quality of functionalism.'[35]

The Courage golden cockerel derived from the ancient coat-of-arms of the Courage family and a full relief model was used in various sizes on the exteriors of the company's houses, on projecting signs and free-standing sign posts, on the cab roofs of their transport fleet and as decorations inside the pubs. The fighting cockerel mark was incorporated also on the labels for the company's bottled beers and on all promotional material, posters and advertisements. Set on a scarlet background, the golden cockerel provided immediate recognition for the hundred or more hotels and public houses owned by the company. These brightly lit signs contrasted with the coaching blue house fascias which carried a distinctive letterform based on Perpetua Bold in gold leaf.

In November 1950, *Art and Industry* ran an article reviewing Milner Gray's design work, including his heraldic devices, trademarks and symbols. In this, George Butler, Art Director of J. Walter Thompson, said:

'Conditions for the artist in advertising have changed a good deal in the last 25 years . . . One of the first artists to realize that many modern designing tasks are beyond the powers of the individual artist working alone, and can best be tackled by a small group of diverse specialists working together on a more or less equal footing, was Milner Gray . . .

'To the world outside the profession, Milner Gray himself first became known as an illustrator . . . But, since the war, Gray has given much of his time to industrial design. His success in this field is due not only to his precision of mind and habit of hard work, but also to a certain human quality apparent in even the most abstract of his work, in his trademarks and the design of those articles which are decorative as well as useful. In spite of his firm belief in teamwork, he has been sensible enough to retain his identity as an individual creative artist.

'Gray has done much more than his share in helping his fellow artists in industry. He has taken a leading part in creating the machinery which for the first time has removed from the artists in industry the handicap of having to act alone in his business dealings. As an artist himself, Gray's achievement in matching his work with his ideals, maintained through 30 very productive years, has played no small part in discouraging the bad and encouraging the good in commercial and industrial art.'

JOHN MALTBY

Gray's work on the corporate identity programme for Courage & Co., developed between 1949 and 1956, covered all aspects of their visual identity. Collaborating designers on exterior and interior treatment of the premises were Peter Moro, Ronald Ingles and John Brucklund.

JOHN MALTBY

JOHN MALTBY

Gray, himself, in the same year, writing a letter to the editor of *The Domestic Equipment Trader*, said, 'From the point of view of the retail store buyer, I feel sure that "good design" can be translated very simply as "a quick-selling line". And perhaps to this definition the buyer would want to make the important addition – "a good repeat line". In other words, from the buyer's point of view, good design is design that the public likes at first sight, and likes also after use and due consideration. Good design sells and goes on selling.

'In order to be very uncontroversial, I go to China for an example of what, by definition is indisputably good design. I attach a photo of a Chinese rice bowl made in a Canton factory last year, 1949, when this factory produced between $3\frac{1}{2}$ and 4 million of these bowls. The original design for the bowl dates from, I think, some-where around 2500 BC. A very popular line this. And quite a good repeat line, too. I wonder whether anything I design in my lifetime will be repeating between $3\frac{1}{2}$ and 4 million a year in 4450 years from now – in the year 6400 AD?'

Stoneware jugs designed by Gray as part of the Courage scheme.

The Festival of Britain

Even before 'Britain Can Make It', discussions had begun about a far more important proposal: an international exhibition to mark the centenary of the Great Exhibition of 1851. The original public idea for this was made by the late Sir Gerald Barry in an open letter to Sir Stafford Cripps published in 1945 in the *News Chronicle*. A year later, a drawing was published in *The Ambassador* showing an earlier scheme by Misha Black for using the derelict South Bank of the Thames for such an international fair. But it was to be another four years before all the proposals and counter proposals and a multitude of committees had arrived at a final plan for a scaled-down national exhibition designed to demonstrate to the world Britain's confidence in her future as an industrial nation. 'The Festival of Britain' became the greatest single stimulus to experiment and creativity in architecture and design that the country had ever experienced. Never before had so many designers come together to work for a common aim, and seldom had they been given such an opportunity to explore new design ideas in a bold expression of 20th century idealism.

By 1947 a design group had been appointed to plan the exhibition in outline. This was led by Sir Hugh Casson and included James Holland, James Gardner, Ralph Tubbs and Misha Black. By 1949 it was finally agreed to use the south bank site after practically every other possibility had been considered and rejected. Soon after this a master plan was approved and detailed design work began.

The site was divided in two by the arches of the Hungerford Bridge and this feature, in conjunction with the irregular shape of the site, led the panel to decide on an informal arrangement of buildings, instead of the classical avenues arranged in a geometric pattern which had been characteristic of the 1937 Paris exhibition and other international fairs.

The Hungerford Bridge provided a natural division of the site into 'upstream' and 'downstream' areas for organisational purposes. Sir Hugh Casson, as architect, James Gardner, as designer, and R. T. James, as engineer, were responsible for co-ordinating the downstream area while the upstream area was supervised in the same way by Misha Black, Ralph Tubbs, James Holland and Ralph Freeman.

For DRU, like so many other design offices at the time, designing for the Festival was an overwhelming preoccupation for two or three years before the opening on 3 May 1951. Under Black's overall direction, Kenneth Bayes led a team of nine designers who prepared all the displays for the inside of Ralph Tubbs' 'Dome of Discovery'; and Alexander Gibson, who joined the Unit in 1948, designed the Regatta Restaurant, the most important architectural job that had been carried out by DRU at that time. Gibson also co-operated with the War Office and the LCC's Chief Engineer on a Bailey bridge for pedestrians beside the Hungerford Bridge.

Signposting

On the graphic side, Milner Gray and Robin Day were responsible for the overall signposting scheme for the exhibition. This work entailed a detailed and comprehensive report on every aspect of signposting for the entire exhibition, of which Gray later said, 'The one thing we had learnt from the Ministry of Information was how to write reports.'

The work also involved choosing all the type faces, and the shape of the signs and signposts, and this too required careful planning:

'Consideration has been given to the evolution of visual symbols for each of the purposes to be served, which would be sufficiently recognisable without the addition of descriptive wording; but

*One of the free-standing signposts which formed part of the general
signposting scheme for the Festival of Britain. Designed by Gray and Robin
Day FSIAD.*

it is felt that in the short period in which these will be before the individual visitor to the exhibition, they could not become sufficiently familiar, however apparently representational they might be. It is proposed, therefore, that each symbol should carry its descriptive title in English. It is not considered necessary that this should be given in other languages (except perhaps where the symbols are illustrated in catalogues or at the entrance of the exhibition, etc.) nor would it be easy to discriminate as to which two or three languages might be used if this were contemplated.

'It is proposed, however, to make use of both colours and simple shapes to impress certain purposes which can be grouped under general heads, such, for instance, as "hygiene" or "refreshments" and thus to assist in the quick and easy recognition of the venue of these services. Of the individual identifying symbols the aim has been to reduce these to the simplest, as well as the most easily recognisable terms. To achieve this the temptation to elaborate the designs has been resisted; the first purpose of these signs must be functional, any leaning towards the unusual, or the more exciting and extravagant display techniques is likely to militate against this purpose. The exhibition without doubt will make full use of such design treatments in other quarters. Where accepted forms such as the word EXIT could be used, these have therefore been used, and rely only on colour and general style to fit them in to the contemporary exhibition scheme. At the same time within these desiderata every effort has been made to make the symbols both interesting in themselves and of good design. Certain of these, such as those dealing with "refreshment" can reasonably be more elaborate, and even light-hearted, in this respect, than those dealing with emergency or more prosaic subjects. The scheme allows for a standard colour and shape

to characterise generic purposes, together with a recognisable symbol in each shape to establish specific purposes.' (For further details about the use of colour see Appendix A, page 85.)

For siting, they advocated that:

'These signs will serve two allied functions, firstly to guide the visitor to the nearest particular venue, and secondly sited at the venue itself, to name and draw attention to it.

'When serving the first of these purposes, as a direction sign, the symbol will in each case be incorporated within a circle [the Group 3 directional shape in Appendix A] and will be equipped with an arrow or pointer to direct to the nearest particular venue. It is proposed that allowance should be made for these direction arrows to be produced as separate units and fitted individually to adjust these to the necessary direction.

'Consideration will need to be given to the method of display of these signs which may be direct on existing wall surfaces or may call for the design of appropriate brackets or free-standing standards designed to carry one of a series of direction signs . . . It is also suggested that certain of the colour schemes and treatments proposed for these signs might be incorporated in the decoration of the actual pavilions or structures concerned as, for instance, the use of reversed blue and white hexagons in the decorative schemes applied to Ladies' and Gentlemen's toilets, thus further facilitating quick and easy recognition . . .'

For execution, they advised:

'It is likely that the most satisfactory way of reproducing the circular directional signs would be by enamelled plate or lithographed aluminium sheet. It seems probably that in view of the comparatively short life required that it would be possible to avoid framing these. The size will need to be considered more carefully in relation to the proposed settings, but a size approximating to that of the current standard bus and coach signs would seem to be suitable, say about 20″ diameter. The hanging signs at the point of venue might be executed in flat relief by means of cut out and imposed wood sections on framed wood panels. Alternatively, as already proposed, in appropriate cases, these might be in full relief modelled in wood, concrete or fibrous plaster.'

The Society of Industrial Artists and Designers were also involved with the Festival of Britain, and James Holland has written of this:

'It has been suggested that the 1951 Festival of Britain is more realistically seen as a summary of the 'thirties and 'forties than as a signpost to the future. Far from offering a new vision and new values in terms of architecture, industrial and graphic design, it was the culminating demonst-ration of attitudes and styles that had first developed in the late 'thirties as, for example, in the manifestations of the MARS group. The impact on the public at large was certainly to give a coherence to the many disconnected indications that something had been happening in the world of environmental design, but the architects and designers chiefly responsible for the Festival presentation had been in practice in pre-war years and in many cases had already established reputations before 1939.'[36]

The Festival and its many off-shoots have been well documented elsewhere, in particular by Mary Banham and Bevis Hillier in *A Tonic to the Nation*.[37] The SIA's involvement was for the most part indirect, through the many members working at various levels on the various projects. On their behalf it was able to negotiate design fees.

The significance of the Festival in the history of the Society must be in the opportunities it gave so many of its members to demonstrate the part that the designer could play in industry and in the community, and that there was no lack of native skill available.

Another Festival of Britain sign, 1951.

ALFRED CRACKNELL

The glass screen at the entrance to the Royal Box, Royal Festival Hall. Designed by Milner Gray in 1951, the rendering of the Royal coat-of-arms was executed on the reverse side of the screen in brilliant cutting, wheel cutting and stone cutting being deeply engraved into the 5/16" thick glass; together with various toned acid treatments in light relief to achieve an appearance of modelling of the heraldic elements of the design. The screen was executed by the London Sand Blast Decoration Glass Works Ltd, at those works Milner Gray is seen inspecting the engraving stage.

DRU and Further Corporate Identity Schemes

'The Affluent Society'

The American magazine *Look*, in a special issue published in 1959, described the decade which was then drawing to a close as 'The fabulous Fifties'. 'America,' it said, 'enters an age of everyday elegance.'

The people of the States had never before experienced such economic prosperity, and many Europeans looked enviously at the technological marvels that were coming out of American factories, or were being presented in exhibitions as a way of life which was only just around the corner. It was a period of dream kitchens, where the housewife was shown at her control centre keeping an eye on the family through a television screen, pushing buttons which selected cameras in different parts of the house, provided automatic meals or instructed the robot floor-cleaning device to go into action. Cars became longer and sleeker and created a new imagery of status and power. It was a world in which it was thought that happiness could be found in possessions, and the possessions were brighter, bigger and more modern in America than anywhere else.

This at least was the impression among those in Britain whose horizons in the early 1950s were being modestly widened by an unfamiliar freedom to buy as many eggs as they wanted. Festival year had marked the end of rationing, but durable consumer goods were slow to appear in sufficient quantities to provide the public with much choice.

Time-Life and Gilbeys

The Festival had tempted DRU, like other design offices, to an over-expenditure on time and effort which sapped its resources. The administrative complexity of what had been the biggest co-ordinated exhibition design project of all time had also complicated the work of the unit, which found itself dealing with numerous government departments and other bodies. For three years, planning and design work for the Festival had taken priority over most other work and, as opening day drew nearer, everything had to be sacrificed to the over-riding need to get the job finished on time. The number of staff of DRU had risen to 40 to cope with this volume of work, but the sudden hiatus after the opening of the exhibition left the unit dangerously weak from a financial point of view.

Fortunately, this did not last long. In 1952, DRU was asked to take part in a scheme which introduced an entirely new sense of affluence, if not to the general public at least to the business world: the interiors of a new building in Bond Street designed by Michael Rosenauer for Time-Life. Sir Hugh Casson and Misha Black again worked together to co-ordinate the design, and they brought in some of Britain's leading designers to work with them on specific areas – Leonard Manasseh, Neville Condor, Robin Day, Neville Ward and others.

Milner Gray was not involved with Time-Life but, in 1953, through the influence of Col. Anthony Grinling, he was appointed Design Consultant to W & A Gilbey Ltd., and this was to be almost an apotheosis for all Gray's work. While work for Tate & Lyle, commissioned the following year, demonstrated what could be done to brighten amorphous packaging, Gray's work for Gilbey's took the use of scripts, the use of craft-based lettering, the use of typefaces and the use of colour and line through to a new level of refinement.

Not since the time of Hadank, who had inspired Milner Gray when he was a young man, had there been such variety and exquisite, decorative use of typography. Art students were inspired, buyers of wine were inspired and Gilbeys won an award from the Royal Society of Arts.

Gilbeys was then still a family firm and Jasper G. Grinling, who later became managing director, was then a junior member of the firm setting out on his first project.

'When I first began to work for the firm, I was told to set up a purchasing department. I began to buy bottles and labels and that sort of thing, but I thought the design of all these things then on the market was very dull indeed.

'I went to our advertising agents, who were then Pembertons, to talk to them about this problem and they told me: "You should go and meet Milner Gray who works in Park Street." So I went to see Milner and he and Kenneth Lamble designed labels and bottles for a range of sherries. These were such a huge success, we went ahead and re-designed all the other bottles and labels. This led on to a full corporate identity scheme for all Gilbey's goods, lorries, stationery and uniforms.'[38]

Gilbeys had a history of good design. Established in 1857, they changed offices four times in the early years to keep pace with their expanding business. The search for suitable accommodation was solved for a long period by an office in Oxford Street (the famous Pantheon) and bond, bottling and distilling facilities in early Victorian ex-railway premises on either side of the Regents Canal in Camden Town. The head office in Oxford Street served its purpose for 70 years until it became necessary (so as to be closer to the production centre) to build the first Gilbey House in 1937, adjoining the bottle warehouse in Camden Town. This building was designed by Serge Chermayeff.

Another change was essential by 1960 when, with six different production buildings and out-of-date warehousing, modern methods of handling could not be introduced. The only answer was a completely fresh start and a decision was made to build in Harlow. The architects for

Gilbey House at Harlow were Peter Falconer, John Timpson and Alexander Gibson of DRU. Alexander Gibson later designed the interiors of the International Distillers and Vintners (IDV) Group London office at York Gate, Regents Park, a group in which Gilbeys became a partner in 1962.

Interior Design for March 1965 wrote about this, 'The building consists of four floors, the upper three of which are given over almost entirely to spacious and well-equipped private offices. On the ground floor are a large general office, a staff canteen and various service areas such as the post-room; there is also a large lift-lobby cum entrance hall. The planning on the upper floors is simple – a central corridor with offices on both sides . . .'

The Royal Society of Arts gave Gilbeys a presidential medal for design management for the work completed to May 1965. This was received by Jasper G. Grinling, as Managing Director in charge of the work. In his speech of thanks, he emphasised four truths which he felt to be essential to good design management:

1 It was vital that the design director should work to a personal conviction.
2 Good design is indivisible – it should extend to all the activities of a firm.
3 A first-class external designer should be employed by a firm's committee of one person only.
4 Good design is no more than one facet of good management.

Milner Gray also carried out a special commission for Gilbeys, travelling with Jasper Grinling to France. Here Gray made a drawing of Chateau Loudenne, 40 miles from Bordeaux, for use on the label of the chateau-bottled wine: this label is still in use.

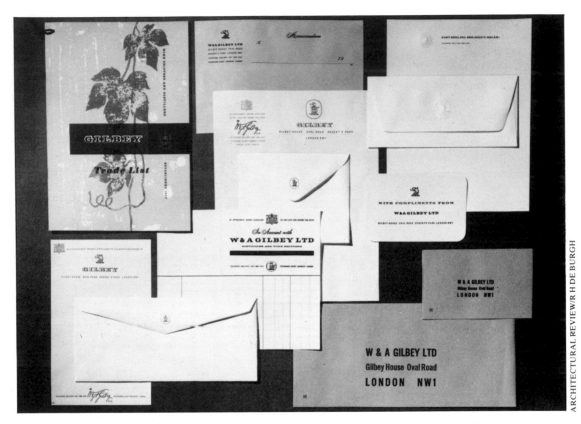

Some of the elements of Gray's work for Gilbeys. The stationery was designed with W M de Majo and the shipping packs with Kenneth Lamble.

JOHN MALTBY

Bottles, labels and an exhibition stand designed by Gray as part of the Gilbeys scheme, and (below) Jasper Grinling.

JOHN MALTBY

JOHN MALTBY

DRU move

In 1958, Design Research Unit, who had moved from Park Street to larger offices at Duke Street, had to move again to even larger premises in a small factory in Aybrook Street, just off Marylebone High Street, which they converted into offices. For this they needed financial backing and turned to IDV for help. IDV agreed and became controlling shareholders of DRU. Jasper Grinling joined the DRU Board of which Milner Gray was the Chairman, and this situation continued until 1972, when Grand Metropolitan took over IDV. When this was proposed, ARCUK, the Architects' Registration Council of the United Kingdom, advised DRU that they were in danger of losing their independence and becoming staff designers of Grand Metropolitan.

The partners' reaction to this was 'We must buy ourselves out to keep our independence!' So a new partnership came into being on 5 October 1974. The relationship with Jasper Grinling and IDV then faded and IDV employed their own staff designer. In 1979, DRU moved to another set of offices in Lower Marsh, Waterloo.

The SIA in the 1950s

Throughout this period, Milner Gray continued to be deeply involved with the work of the SIA. By the beginning of 1953, the society had set up 13 specialist groups to represent the various fields of practice of the membership and was prepared to re-examine its structure in the light of this group development. Proposals were put to the annual general meeting that two main groups, the general commercial design executive and the general industrial design executive should be set up to form the governing council of the society plus such other groups covering the various specialist interests of the SIA as might be determined by council. The relationship of

general to specialist groups was that the two main groupings formed as the council were termed 'the Industrial Design Executive' and 'the Commercial Design Executive'. This worked very well during the earlier recruiting period but the division later began to pose a threat to the whole existence of the organisation which was, in intention, dedicated to representing designers in all fields of work.

At the extraordinary general meeting that following the AGM of 1953, Milner Gray proposed the Council's recommendation to members to amend the constitution to provide for a multi-group structure to replace the existing two-group structure and, after much discussion, an amended version of the proposal was agreed.

The society was outstanding in giving time to organising seminars, conferences and social occasions for its members and for many years an annual conference was held in Chipping Camden, always including a visit to the home of Sir Gordon Russell at 'Kingcombe'. Speakers included Stevie Smith, the poetess; Richard Gregory, author of *Eye and Brain*[39]; Professor Gilbert Ryle, author of *The Concept of Mind*[40]; and Professor Meredith Thring, author of *Man, Machines and Tomorrow*.[41]

The society's 25th birthday fell in 1955. In an interview, Milner Gray remembered:

'I played some part in the swinging of the thing round to such matters as education and protection. A proper system of education is the keynote of any profession and it still hasn't got going . . . 25 years later. I tried to widen the field. Paul Nash took on the Presidency and the Council included Allan Walton, Serge Chermayeff, Ted Kauffer, Frank Dobson and Graham Sutherland . . . it's surprising how much the general world of commercial art was a free-for-all then.'[42]

Further corporate identity schemes

In 1955, Milner Gray became joint design consultant with Misha Black to the De La Rue group of companies. He wrote of this in *Lettering for Architects and Designers*:

'In the case of an organisation with such widely differing interests as the Thomas De La Rue Group of Companies, the establishment of a corporate identity programme calls for emphasis on divisional identification within the concept of an overall design policy. The company's activities embrace the production of bank notes and postage stamps, the manufacture of plastic laminates and extrusions, of gas- and oil-fired heating and cooking appliances (this division was later hived off) and the printing of playing cards and stationers' sundries. A house symbol was devised, featuring a silhouette head of the founder of the firm, to form a visual link between the four main divisions of the company. Individual identification of divisions was achieved by the use of characteristic letter-forms and colours. For the company's head office and for their security division, it was decided to adopt an improved version of the traditional Gothic letterform long associated with De La Rue, and to use as a secondary typeface Engravers Roman. For other divisions and subsidiary companies, contrasting typefaces were used. The familiar green of the English banknote inspired the adoption of Fir Green as the company's basic house colour.

'The company's head office and showrooms in Regent Street were designed in conformity with the approved house style. The improved Gothic name style has been used on the main fascia of the front elevation in white vitreous enamelled metal letters set out on distance pieces from a black granite background. To ensure maximum legibility, over the entrance doors at a lower level, the secondary letterform, Engravers Roman, has been adopted as being easier to read than the Gothic characters. These letters are in white on a dark green background.

'An internally lit projecting box sign utilises the Gothic lettering with engrossed flourishes as a decorative embellishment. This treatment of the name is also used in other settings.

'The new symbol was especially modelled for manufacture as a set of cameos by Josiah Wedgewood & Sons in their famous Jasper ware and incorporated as a centre boss to the black bronze door handles at the main entrance to De La Rue House.

'The complete range of company stationery and complementary printed material for the company, its divisions and subsidiaries was re-designed in conformity with the agreed house style. Central and departmental head office letter-headings are die-stamped and printed in the dark green house colour.

'The whole of the De La Rue's transport fleet has been brought into line with the company's new face. Their Austin 3-ton FC chassis vans are finished in dark green, with the house symbol in white and the standard treatment of the company name in gold leaf.'[43]

In 1955 Milner Gray also became design consultant to James Joblings Ltd for Pyrex oven-to-table glassware. These were made in heat-resisting pressed glass and had smooth profiles to facilitate emptying and cleaning, together with large and comfortable handles to ensure that they could be carried safely from oven to table.

In the same year Gray became Master of the Faculty of Royal Designers for Industry and a Vice President of the Royal Society of Arts (he was a member of Council from 1959 to 1965). He was also made a member of the Packaging Advisory Council of the Printing and Allied

The external projecting lettered sign designed by Gray and Ronald Armstrong for (below) Thomas de la Rue company's premises in Regent Street (Architects: Misha Black, Alexander Gibson, and Philip Lucey) together with packaging and stationery, designed by Gray.

Trades Research Association (a post he held until 1964). He was made a member of the Formation Committee of the International Council of Societies of Industrial Design in 1956 and went to Halsingborg for their first International Design Congress where he made a speech entitled 'The Designer's Dilemma'. He wrote an article for the Royal Society of Arts Journal about the ICSID Congress called 'Halsingborg Puts Out More Flags'. He also attended the second international conference in Stockholm in 1959.

JOHN MALTBY

ICSID meeting at the Royal Institute of British Architects in June 1957. Gray and Werner Graeff (Germany) discuss the agenda.

Packaging

In 1956 Milner Gray wrote a paper on packaging entitled 'A Brave Lot O' String, the problems of a package designer'. This was read before the Double Crown Club on 8 February 1956.

'My father was a dab at doing up parcels, and, as children, we would stand by and admire the skilful fold of paper and deft knotting of the

Part of a range of shapes for casseroles, roasting dishes, fruit and cereal bowls in Pyrex oven-to-table glass. Designed for Joblings of Sunderland by Gray and Kenneth Lamble in 1955, together with Gray's new trade-mark for Pyrex.

string, especially round about Christmas time when there were so many packages to be done up. Whether this may have influenced me in later years, I leave to the psychologists. But unlike the Exmoor farmer's wife who used 'a brave lot o' string' to make sure of the Michaelmas goose, my father was a tidy-minded man, his parcels were models of a neat and scientific economy.

'A part of the art of designing packages is to achieve the desired effect with an economy of means. In this the package designer pursues a well-worn path familiar to artists practising in other spheres, but he works with a set of tools peculiar to his trade and to conditions more circumscribed than some more personal forms of art expression. Most of us at some time have looked with something of wonder at the apparent simplicity of effort with which some favourite draughtsman or painter has affected us, be he a Thurber, a Holbein or a Matisse. Some part perhaps is magic, the magic of a subconscious assessment of form and character; but a great part, like the nimble hand of the magician, is the result of knowledge of his craft and long practice.

'So it is with the package designer, who must have a wide general knowledge of packaging materials, of their comparative costs and their relative properties; of the machines and processes which translate these materials into containers of all kinds; of filling and packing plant and methods; and, above all, of the needs and desires of men and women comprising the markets of the world, who will ultimately buy or reject the packaged product. But with this difference from some other artists, that he does not work alone. However small it may be, no one man can design a package in the same sense that no one man designs any article produced in quantity by machine. It is the product of the experience of a team, in the case of the package,

composed of the manufacturer, with his intimate knowledge of his own goods; of the packaging material supplier, with the technical information on his particular type of container; and of the designer whose job it is to co-ordinate this various experience, adding his own gift for its visual and tactile interpretation . . . If he is worth his fee, the designer is first and foremost an artist, one who is sensitive to the atmosphere of the product and to the mood of the consumer in buying it; and his vital contribution is the aesthetic character which he brings to his work.'

Watneys

Following completion of his consultancy for Courage in 1956, Milner Gray was invited to become design consultant to the Watney-Mann Group of companies for a corporate identity and public house identification programme. For many years the name WATNEYS in bold block Gill Sans capitals on the fascias and signs of public houses had been a familiar sight, particularly in and around London. These inscriptions, and the sign of the Red Barrel adopted in 1935, displayed to the general public a face plain and unmistakable enough. But, as the firm expanded and absorbed smaller breweries outside London, each with its own distinctive style, the question began to be asked: Was 'Gill Sans' the right style of lettering for country districts? This led to further questions: Was it, in fact, the right lettering for London or did it, despite its clarity, spell out a rather cold, cheerless welcome on public house fascias and over bar entrance doors?

Following a survey of a selection of typical town and country houses owned by the company, a programme was devised and adopted which aimed at achieving effective house identification, without submerging the individual character of each house or its suitability to its surroundings. The prime aim of this programme was to effect a break-away from the rather frigid atmosphere of public house architecture, furnishings and accessories, developed in the years between the wars, and to re-establish the atmosphere of comfort and conviviality epitomised in Dr Johnson's testimonial that '. . . there is nothing which has yet been contrived by man by which so much happiness is produced as by a good tavern or inn'.

A number of public houses, divided into typical architectural style-groups, were nominated for experimental decoration in conformity with proposals for an improved house style, which was also explored in relation to the treatment of the company's transport fleet, labels, stationery, advertising material and bar accessories. In its essentials, this comprehensive design programme involved the adoption of a standard logotype for the name WATNEYS; the application of a group of five secondary letter-forms for use for specified purposes; the standardisation of the company's Red Barrel trade-mark; the use of certain subsidiary decorative features including borders and end pieces based on a hop and barley motif; the adoption of specified colours for the painting of wall surfaces, fascias, signs and noticeboards, and the introduction of basic house colours for print and publicity purposes.

To ensure the consistent interpretation of the approved scheme in the decoration of the company's properties, a house identification manual was compiled for the use of the company's surveyors departments who were responsible for the continued carrying out of the house identification programme. The manual included references for all paintwork colours to be used, square-up alphabets of the approved lettering styles and decorative features, and particular attention was drawn to the essential need for good sign-writing. Where applicable, applied letters cut from plastic sheet, hardboard

Elements of the house style for Watney Mann.

Cut out letters for the Watneys scheme.

The Whittaker Arms.

The Cock and Lion, Wigmore Street, London.

or plywood were recommended to ensure conformity of letterforms to the standard.

Beer bottle labels and printed cans conformed to the all-embracing house style. The retention of the old label colours and of the oval as the predominant shape in the new labels was carried out to keep a close link with the old familiar style. The oval, however, was super-imposed on a rectangular shaped label as an aid to more accurate positioning by mechanical labelling than is possible with an oval shaped label.

At every stage in the development of this programme, the danger of over-standardisation was recognised and the manual included photo-prints of typical houses to illustrate how these basic elements had been used in varying combi-nations to achieve variety within an over-riding unity of style.

Other work in the 1950s

In 1957, Milner Gray was Chairman of the panel of judges for the first Council of Industrial Design Awards for 'Designs of the Year'. On this panel were Professors Robert Goodden and Richard D. Russell, Brian O'Rorke, the architect, and Mrs Astrid Sampe. They picked out twelve outstandingly simple and practical objects: dinner and teaware, table glasses, wallpaper, cutlery, and curtain fabric, a carpet, plastic tableware, a lamp shade, a TV set, a convertible settee-bed, Pyrex casseroles (designed by Gray who withdrew for this deci-sion) and a convector open fire.

Oriana

During these years DRU continued to win a series of major interior design commissions. Another all-absorbing assignment with which Milner Gray was actively involved was a commission to co-ordinate the interior design of the 40000 ton passenger ship 'Oriana'. Towards the end of 1955, Milner Gray and Sir Colin Anderson, a neighbour and a director of the Orient line, met by chance on Hampstead tube station. Sir Colin mentioned that a new ship was being planned and asked whether DRU would be interested in acting as design co-ordinators. It was well-known to the design world that Brian O'Rorke, a fellow RDI, had acted for Orient on the internal, and to some extent the external, design of the company's five previous ships. Sir Colin explained that as the size of their ships increased it had become apparent that their complexities demanded a larger design team and one with particular experience in large scale design co-ordination and this was his reason for turning to DRU. It would be a requirement that O'Rorke's services should be retained as consultant and that he should undertake the design of some areas; and R. D. Russell had already been commissioned to design the passenger cabins.

Milner discussed these requirements with Misha Black and after further meetings DRU received a five-and-a-half page brief entitled 'The Problem'. After meeting with O'Rorke and holding various internal discussions, DRU wrote to Sir Colin commenting on the brief and proposing fees. On 3 May, DRU were confirmed as design co-ordinators. Michael Middleton has said, of this:

'The following months were occupied with clarification of the design and procedural issues involved. The first need was for the senior members of DRU who were concerned to familiarise themselves with the technical, func-

SS Oriana's badge symbolizing the link between the first and second Elizabethan eras.

tional and human factors that might affect the design problem ahead . . .'[44]

By September 1957, at Barrow-in-Furness, ship no. 1061, later to be named the 'Oriana', had been laid down. Programming the work for this was a complex operation. The ship builders initiated progress schedules which were finally agreed in consultation with DRU. Design policy was established through a steering committee. This proved an effective method by which the designers could first be briefed and then obtain approval of the decorative schemes for each space. This worked smoothly. By April 1959, a list of decorating contractors had been drawn up

A detail from the Junior Club (first class) showing one of the decorative murals in Wareite designed by Robert Perritt of DRU.

Decorative plaque wrought in aluminium anodised in gun-metal, gold and silver, with photographically engraved figures.

and four contractors appointed.

On 3 November 1959, Oriana was christened and launched by HRH Princess Alexandra. At this stage no fitting out of the public rooms had as yet been started on site. The complex furnishing and decorative schemes were finally completed and SS Oriana sailed on her maiden voyage on 3 December 1960.

In addition to serving on the steering committee, Milner Gray undertook responsibility for the stairways (with individual bas-reliefs on each half-landing by Mary Martin), the main corridors and signposting throughout the ship. To assist passengers in finding their way about

so large a ship, public areas were identified by colours and symbols in addition to directional signposting. Each chosen deck colour was used in the deck floor pattern for an arrow pointing to the bow end of the ship. In this way passengers could tell immediately which deck they were on and which was fore and aft. Milner Gray also designed the ship's badge – a double 'E' symbolising a link between the first and second Elizabethan eras. 'Oriana' was a name attributed to Queen Elizabeth the first and the badge surmounted by an Elizabethan pearl crown and surrounded by an 'O' for Oriana. A special version of the badge was designed for the canal light door on the bows, for which permission was sought and received from Buckingham Palace.

Other work of this period included the Royal Garden Hotel; *The Times* new building; West London Air Terminal; the CIS building in Manchester; new offices for the Alliance Building Society in Brighton; Britannic House and the new headquarters of British Petroleum.

In 1959, Milner Gray became a member of the National Advisory Council on Art Education, a post he held until 1969. He also became Chairman of the SIA Drafting Committee for a 'Syllabus for the Study of Professional Practice in Commercial and Industrial Design'.

In this year, as has been said, DRU moved to Duke Street, between Oxford Street and Wigmore Street where, to encourage the expansion of architectural work, they formed a separate office called Black, Bayes, Gibson & Partners; the partners including Anthony Wilkinson and William Apps who extended the scope to include not only the factories, houses and office buildings undertaken before, but also churches and schools. Possibly the best-known job to come out of these new architectural offshoots was the small mammal house at the London Zoo, designed by Misha Black and Kenneth Bayes in 1961.

Design Research Unit directorate in 1963.

JOHN MALTBY

Design in the 1960s

Milner Gray at Aspen

In 1961, Milner Gray travelled to Aspen, Colorado, as the British delegate speaker at the International Design Conference. There he said to designers in the final summary session:

'. . . the work we most admire is often the simplest and the most obvious – of the kind that we all know we could have done, had we only thought of it. It is simple and inevitable because, the right question having been asked, there was no longer any difficulty in finding the right answer.

'As soon as we tackle a design problem, we, ourselves, become a part of the problem we aim to solve, bringing to its solution our own predilections, which may not coincide with those of others associated with us in its solution. The solution will seldom be achieved by bulldozing our ideas over the other fellow's, who, too, is as identified with the problem as we are.

'I believe that the designer's originative capacity derives from an inward urge to bring new forms into being. His creative contribution differs not in *quality* but in *kind* from that of other industrial workers – the factory manager who evolves a new production-line technique, or the business executive who conceives a new sales system. The designer's originative capacity is not necessarily superior or fundamentally different; the difference lies in his application of it. This, which turns the tolerable into the beautiful, the merely functional into the highly desirable, makes him as valuable to industry as his scientific and executive colleagues. Every design is in a sense an act of communication, a statement of a conviction about the nature and the functions of an article: a statement for which the designer accepts responsibility. The greater the intensity with which he appreciates and the integrity with which he expresses the whole truth about the product as he perceives it, the better his designs.

'Integrity of expression comes from the integration of thought and action, integration of mind, eye and hand, of honest disciplined work. The designer's social contribution and responsibility is to realize the true and total value to the ultimate user of the product he designs.'

He continued, too, with his work for the Society of Industrial Artists. Although proposals submitted by Misha Black concerning changing the society's name seem to have aroused little interest, the word 'Designers' was added to the title of the Society in 1963 and the SIA became the SIAD.

Also in 1963, Milner Gray became Master of the Art Workers' Guild and in 1963–7 was a member of the CoID/GPO Stamp Advisory Committee. He designed and modelled armorial bearings for the Central Electricity Generating Board and, in 1965, was a delegate to the European Packaging Federation Conference in Copenhagen.

In May 1966, the last SIA Journal (no. 159) appeared and the magazine emerged in June under the new banner *Designer*. This was edited by Elizabeth Lowry-Dory.

From 1967 to 1968, Milner Gray became President of the SIAD for a second term. This was no sinecure. It was a time of great upheaval and discussion in the design world where 'the Pop movement' had made a significant impact on the comparatively sterile world of post-war design thinking. It certainly challenged any idea of a 'correct' approach to the aesthetics of design.

Misha Black wrote about this:

'For a short time in Britain the art school ebullience exploded into the high street. Skirts leaped high up thighs, Carnaby Street became a symbol for a release from parental respectability. This image is already tired and tarnished and needs replacement by a new wave of equal transcience.

'The designers who are motivated by irrationality are more closely allied to the fine arts than to industrial design. Their invention is at the outer fringe of art, but they celebrate the unpredictability of man, the instincts which make people climb mountains and make love. But they share one characteristic with the designers of useful three-dimensional objects. This is technical knowledge and skill. Many years of learning and practice are necessary before any designer is able to practise with professional competence and this he or she must have whether they decide to dedicate their skills and creativity to design for intermediate technology or urban transportation, to book design or fashion fabrics . . .

'In our present epoch of social and technological upheaval no industrial designer can have the absolute conviction which justifies flamboyant expressionism. We should, indeed, approach our tasks with humility and accept that we are usually more usefully engaged in making minor improvements to existing products and systems than in radical innovation.'[45]

In his presidential address in 1968 to the SIAD, 'The Price and the Value', Milner Gray said:

'We live in an age in which the winds of change seem to have reached gale force, so fast and fierce do they blow. Our children, when they are being taught at all, outstrip most of us in an understanding of sciences and systems undreamed of by their parents' grandfathers. My own grandfather, though he lived long enough to have seen an aeroplane, would have died before flying in one – as indeed he did! That a computer could perform any part of the task of the clerk wearing paper cuffs and sitting on a high stool at a high desk in his outer office would have been quite beyond his comprehension.

'By the same token, we live of necessity in an age of reappraisal. In what I believe to be a natural craving for law and order, we seek continually to uncover and cure the root causes of our disorders, sometimes I fear with little enough success. Of one thing I am sure: unless we really care about the intrinsic value of what we design, unless we really care about what the products we design look like and feel like and how well they serve the community, we designers cannot claim to be accepted as a professional body of men and women; as a profession actively aware of the needs of the community and skilled in the means of communicating within the community. Communication is someone sending a message and someone receiving it. The act of communicating is, I believe, not confined to graphic concepts; every design is, in a sense, an act of communication as well as of commitment – a declaration of a conviction about the nature and the purpose of an article – or of a message, for which the designer must assume a large share of the responsibility, for this is the designer's special discipline. The greater the clarity with which he perceives and the sincerity which he expressed this conviction, the better will be the design solution to the particular problem in hand.'

British Rail

The big commission for Milner Gray and DRU during this period was the British Railways corporate identity programme which aimed to give the general public a new image of the railways as modern, vigorous and forward-looking. The project had, as its aim, the stimulation of interest and confidence in the service which the railways provided. It also introduced economies and highlighted the improvements in equipment and techniques which had been made or were in progress since the inauguration of a modernisation plan in 1955.

Trophy awarded to Francis Chichester, the winner of the first single-handed Atlantic yacht race in 1960. The trophy was designed by Gray; the case by Ronald Armstrong. The centre of the plate shows the route taken by the winner on a gnomic chart which is engraved with the route in gold damascene.

The travelling gavel for the ICSID designed by Gray and made and presented to ICSID by Mr Geoffrey Dunn.

The idea of consciously trying to improve the public image of British Railways by imposing, wherever possible, a recognisable family like-ness on everything seen and used by the public, began to take shape at an informal meeting early in 1963 between George Williams and John Nuneley of British Railways and Milner Gray. In April 1963, Gray was asked to attend a meeting with executives of British Railways to discuss the implications of devising a new image for the railways system and of programming its implementation. He was subsequently invited to be Chairman of a working party composed jointly of departmental specialists from British Railways and two other DRU partners, Ronald Armstrong and Kenneth Lamble.

From the beginning, the design panel, an advisory body appointed by the British Rail-ways Board in 1956 and chaired by T. H. Summerson, had agreed on its main working policy: that the greater part of the detailed designing for this vast programme should be entrusted to consultant designers working to and with the panel's small qualified staff, which was headed first by Christian Barman until 1962 and then by George Williams, who was a stimulating influence and a great loss when he died in November 1965.

By April 1964, preliminary design proposals for a corporate identity programme prepared by Gray and his DRU design team had been approved in principle by the working party and were presented, first of all, to the design panel with a fully documented scheme for their implementation. These proposals were then submitted to the management committee on 22 July and finally submitted to and approved by the Railways Board on 23 July.

A steering committee, on which Gray and Lamble served, was then appointed to take over from the working party to control the implemen-tation of the principles which had been approved, and to prepare manuals to guide the many departments in the execution and use of the elements of the house style and to ensure the maintenance of standards in every field of application. A film was also made to explain the scheme and the need for administrative procedure to give effect to a planned programme – which then went ahead.

In January 1965, the Design Centre mounted an exhibition designed by DRU under Gray. This showed the work done for British Railways and was entitled 'The New Face of British Railways'. It demonstrated train liveries, uniforms, posters, timetables and other printed matter, scale models of electric trains, examples of station signboards and lettering, cutlery, tableware and furnishings. A section on 'Freight techniques in prospect' illustrated a prototype car-carrier, a tanker for road–rail operation and the liner trains. Architecture, civil engineering and research for the railways were also represented.

The most notable innovations in this scheme were the two-way arrow symbol (designed by Gerald Barney of DRU) and the logotype 'British Rail' (both are currently still in use). Of the arrow it was said 'The double-arrow trademark chosen is forceful, simple and easily recognisable. It is symbolic of the two-way rail service it represents and can be adapted to a variety of applications.'

Of the changing of the name 'British Railways' to 'British Rail', Milner Gray has said:

'. . . this came about in a curious way. When I was exploring possible letter styles, I asked the DRU design team to draw out one or two different letter forms, but I told them it was unnecessary to spell the name out in full. When I saw the shortened name, I thought what a much better title it made and what an advantage this would be in the saving of space in many settings. We all

British Rail corporate identity manuals, with a typical double-spread sheet.

British Rail staff uniforms designed by Gray and Kenneth Lamble in close association with British Rail.

JOHN MALTBY

agreed that this was so and when we put it to the working party they also agreed and it went on to the design panel and to the Board. They liked it, too. How surprised we all were!'

Dr Beeching was Chairman of the British Railways Board at this time. When the scheme was put up to the Board by the working party there was a great deal of discussion – so much that Milner Gray began to wonder whether the scheme would be rejected. But Dr Beeching looked round the room and declared, 'Well, we are all agreed, gentlemen' and, at his word, everything was accepted.

DRU's involvement with British Rail also included design consultancy for seven locomotives by Misha Black. The development of the corporate identity programme, under Milner Gray and the preparation of the design manuals was undertaken by the British Rail design staff headed by George Williams and his deputy Ellis Miles. The corporate identity programme was also, by 1966, extended to Sea Speed hovercraft.

The British Rail scheme was yet another example of Gray's superlative design management. Meticulous in analysing the problem, he was no less so in reporting and implementing his chosen solutions. Even where others were involved in the design, like Gerald Barney, Milner Gray held a tight rein on the carrying out of the work and the devising of manuals saw that the clients, too, did not take decisions that were no part of Gray's plan.

Within DRU, Milner Gray encouraged the development of skills and personality in young designers and saw to it that they did not lack opportunity and that their work was always acknowledged. In this he set an example. He did not ask more, in terms of professionalism, of other designers than he was prepared to demonstrate himself.

A new scheme for Ilford

As has been described, Gray designed a corporate identity programme for Ilford soon after the end of the second world war. But company images don't last for ever. The status of the company, changing marketing conditions, public acceptance or rejection of new forms and new ideas all result in the need to review and, if necessary, to revise an existing image, however, well it may have been originated. So it was with the Ilford Company, who had effected links with CIBA in Switzerland.

In 1966 they turned once again to Gray and DRU for a revised and up-dated corporate identity programme of which they announced in their journal, *Visual*, that it was:

'. . . a new design scheme being introduced by Ilford Limited. It will establish an all-embracing house style by effecting a readily discernible visual link between product presentation, advertising and sales promotion material, publications, the transport fleet, and every other aspect of the company's activities.

'The new design scheme has been produced by a team at Design Research Unit under the guidance of the Ilford consultant designer Milner Gray CBE, RDI, PPSIA, AGI, Hon.DesRCA, and by a small committee comprising Ilford Advertising and Product Services Departments.

'The problems involved were perhaps more detailed and more complex than those of many other organisations. Ilford catalogues list more than 18000 products in various product groups – cameras, films, papers, chemicals, machines – and in addition to these there are the technical publications, instruction leaflets, company magazines, stationery, advertising in all its aspects and transport; all to be brought into the design scheme.

'The requirements were: a distinctive colour

scheme which would stand apart from competitors in all product groups; a typographical style which would give maximum legibility in the crowded conditions of today's retailing; a symbol that would reflect Ilford activities with the colour scheme and typographical style; and then to translate these elements into modern packaging. These ideas were to be linked with those of CIBA, with whom the company were preparing packages for products being jointly marketed in the Common Market countries and Switzerland.

'White and blue were selected as the new house colours, white being chosen for its distinctiveness. Having chosen white as the background colour, it was then possible to rationalise the designs. Black on white with black symbols was to be the design for Ilford black-and-white films, papers and chemicals, supplemented by product colour codes. For colour films, blue and red lettering with red symbols were chosen for colour reversal, and blue and green lettering with green symbols for colour negative. So with each range of products for the various divisions the same rationalisation is applied.'[46]

The scheme for Ilford won one of the five Royal Society of Arts Presidential Awards for Design Management in 1969. 'This award,' commented the RSA award selection committee, 'underlines a point often overlooked even by genuinely design-conscious companies – that design policies or house styles or corporate identities need periodical revision or renewal.'

In 1967, Milner Gray was appointed design consultant to the British Aluminium Co for another corporate identity programme which was completed during the following year.

ICI

In 1968, DRU was commissioned under Gray's direction to prepare a corporate identity scheme for ICI, Britain's biggest commercial enterprise. A joint working party was set up under the chairmanship of A. L. Sumner. The working party's terms of reference were to study and resolve the problems set by:

1 The correct use and application of the ICI roundel.
2 The consistent relationship between the names of the divisions and the company.
3 The unification of the product logotypes and their relationship with the roundel.
4 The use of an ICI colour or colours.
5 The adoption of an ICI alphabet and its application to notice boards and general signing, etc.
6 The design of a basic range of stationery with guidance for a variety of applications.

In addition, the design programme included the preparation of an ICI house style manual embodying the approved visual elements of the house style for the guidance of everyone concerned with its implementation. The working party agreed to collect information, assemble and analyse the information, and make decisions prior to producing a report.

In April 1968, Gray and Armstrong produced a report which resolved the problems set out in the original brief. They recommended that he existing roundel, with minor modifications, should remain, because it was already recognised by the public; they proposed that the firm's house colours should be changed from blue to orange which

'. . . combines well with white, silver or silver-grey [the recommendations for the transport fleet] and with red and yellow (for statutory notices). It projects a warm and contemporary image. It minimises the effect of travel staining.'

JOHN MALTBY

Notices in Wilton Works solvents area as part of the ICI scheme. Designed by Gray in 1966–70.

They recommended 'Helvetica' as a typeface of classic proportions and with enough character to be used on stationery. The report quotes:

'It is available in bold, medium and light weights; this enables us to use the light weight for stationery and the medium weight for nameplates, directional signs, interior and exterior, and on vehicles. On vehicles where advertising slogans are sometimes considered of value, we suggest that these should be written in this style, irrespective of the product logotype style.'

They also put forward a proposal for the design of a house flag. ICI's acceptance of the recommendation was reported to employees in the ICI magazine of January 1969.

Design Research Unit personnel in 1968.

JOHN GARNER

Design in the 1970s

The SIAD

In 1969, HRH the Duke of Edinburgh agreed to become patron of the Society of Industrial Artists and Designers. Milner Gray attended the International Conference of Societies of Industrial Design (ICSID) 6th Assembly and Congress in London. He also became a member of the committee appointed jointly by the British Academy and the Royal Commission for the Exhibition of 1951 to '. . . review the activities of the British School of Rome'.

In 1970, he designed armorial bearings and a common seal for the Post Office and, in the same year, was a speaker at the Design Council conference on 'Corporate identity – its organisation and management.'

In 1972 he was a delegate to another Design Council conference on 'The Management of Design for the European Markets' and also became a member of a Standing Joint Committee for the SIAD and the Design Council. He designed a badge for the Balmoral Estate Ranger Service and, once again, from 1973 to 1975, became design consultant to Courage & Co for the re-evaluation and updating of their public house identification.

From 1973 to 1977, Gray was Chairman of the SIAD Charter Working Party. This work led to the granting of a Royal Charter to the Society. This charter was a most important step in the development of the Society, giving it the status that Gray and his colleagues had dreamed of in the '20s when the Society was first set up. It confirmed the SIAD as the one authoritative body for designers and SIAD members found that the government and industry began to take notice of what the Society said. Thus, Gray had lived to see social and political status given to designers and, in recognition of this, it was decided to re-name the annual design oration 'The Milner Gray Lecture'.

In 1976, Gray designed an official emblem for the Queen's Silver Jubilee for use in street decoration and souvenirs. He also acted as design consultant for station decorations for British Rail.

Again in 1976, he spoke to the Royal Society of Arts on 'Packaging Progress', talking about technical advances since the war, the importance of visual appeal, the effect of sociological changes and the use of plastics.

1977 was a tragic year for the design world. Five well loved and respected members of the SIAD died: Sir Basil Spence, a Fellow of the Society; Lilian Hockwell, a founder member and signatory of the original articles of association in 1930; Hulme Chadwick, the SIAD's 18th President; Lynton Lamb, a great liberal thinker; and Sir Misha Black. Sir Misha's death, on 11 August, ended the partnership with Milner Gray that had continued, unbroken, since 1932.

Milner Gray at 80

Gray reached his 80th birthday two years later. 'Happy birthday Milner', ran a headline in *Designer*.

'We pay tribute here to Milner Gray whose 80th birthday falls this month. Milner has been involved in the Society's affairs, without interruption, since he helped to found it in 1930. He has held a number of offices including the Presidency (twice) and is currently Chairman of the Trustee Board. To his other honours – CBE, RDI, AGI – was recently added an Honorary Doctorate of the Royal College of Art. To mark this occasion, and the Society's 50th anniversary, Graham Sutherland, himself an old friend of Milner's and closely associated with the Society in its early days, has done a portrait of Milner which will hang in its premises.'

The Sunday Telegraph magazine discussed the importance of this portrait after Sutherland's death, a few months later:

'Sutherland leaves behind an affectionate memento. One of the last portrait commissions painted by the late Graham Sutherland goes on show at London's Arts Club next week. It shows a Pickwickian-looking gentleman with brilliant shining eyes and a puckish expression.

'"It is obviously a portrait done with love," said a member of the body which commissioned it. That is not something which has been said about all Mr Sutherland's portraits . . . But this one is rather special. The subject is Mr Milner Gray who is just 80 years old and is the doyen of the world of industrial design. He is the last surviving member of the group of people who, in 1930, founded what is now the Society of Industrial Artists and Designers.

'Sutherland, who was commissioned by London Transport and Shell before the Second World War, was a member of the Society, and served for a while on its governing council. In view of this it was decided to ask him to do a portrait in honour of the Society's jubilee. The quoted fee for a Sutherland portrait at the time was around £10000. As the SIAD only had £1000 to spend, the governing council asked for a drawing rather than a painting. But when Sutherland heard that Milner Gray was to be the subject, he said he would do it for £1000 anyway.

'"We were students at Goldsmiths' College in south London together" Mr Gray explains. "I had digs in a nice little Queen Anne house in Blackheath. And when I heard that Graham was looking for a room I managed to persuade my landlady to give him one of the spare bedrooms. I had a sitting room and he shared that. It was there that he set up his etching press and made an easy name for himself turning out

work for the engraving boom that was raging through the art world at that time. He stayed on with me until he married a girl from Goldsmiths', Kathleen, and went off to live in a Kent village. Later, when he and his wife moved into a bigger house in Kent, they needed someone to help fill all their space, so I moved in with them. They used to call me The Lodger. By then I had founded my own design partnership and was commuting up to London every day."'[47]

In July, 1979, Milner Gray spoke at the convocation of the Royal College of Art. Speaking on behalf of Sir Cecil Beaton, Edwardo Paolozzi, James Sterling and himself, Gray said:

'Mr Provost, Mr Rector, Friends and Members of the College, the honour of speaking on behalf of the new Doctors Honoris Cuasa has fallen to me, I was told, because of my long association with the College; indeed I can think of no other reasonable justification for having been chosen.

'My first tenuous link with the Royal College of Art was when, in the very early 1920s, I came to convocation as an art student visitor from another College, and I recall vividly, despite the passage of years, how impressed I was, as well as surprised, by the sight of fellow art students bedecked in cap and gown, though nothing so gorgeous as the gowns and hoods we now assume.

'We dreamt and talked and even wrote, in those far off days, of the establishment of a Chair in design at some university, but sadly accepted the aspiration as an unrealisable dream.

'Later I taught briefly in the Graphic Design School until the College was whisked away to Westmorland for the duration of World War Two and I elsewhere. And the dream remained a dream.

JOHN MALTBY

Milner Gray speaking at the convocation of the Royal College of Art, July 1979.

'Much later still I was privileged to serve on the College Council in the stimulating Darwinian epoch when my good, though sometimes bewildering friend Robin, raised the College to University status, settled us in this building, which so rightly bears his name, and one early dream became a reality and more.

'Now, after seven years of Lord Esher's wise leadership, having entered a yet third epoch, we already witness the first fruits of Dick Guyatts' able and experienced control, and here stand I before you in goodly company and in doctor's guise, benefited by Senate's mid-year honours list. However, I live in the hope that, despite my doctorate, such patients as still attend my surgery will have no cause to castigate me in the terms of the old song, "When a man's sick he makes a fuss, calls in a doctor who makes him wuss". But these are foolish things to the all-wise and I love Wisdom more than She loves me.

'The role of the artist–designer in the dual, but I believe wholly one, practice of art and design – the pursuit of ideal form as a means of communication or the perfection of function — is as old as the cave drawings of Altimara or the invention of the wheel; but the methodical study and the means of assessment of art and design at University level is something in which this Royal College of Art has led the way.

'Every exercise in the visual arts, as well as being the expression of an inward urge to create new forms, is in one sense an act of communication – in painting the statement of a conviction about the nature of things we see, and in the field of design a declaration of a conviction about the nature and purpose of an artefact or a message, for which the designer must assume a large share, but not the whole, of the responsibility, for the practice of design is generally a team job. The greater the clarity with which he expresses his conviction, the better will be the ultimate solution.

'Let us never forget that behind the cap and gown, the degree and diploma, the pomp and ceremony of Convocation lies the simple and age-old instinctive urge of the artist to create something worthwhile. Whether you are painting the ceiling of the Sistine Chapel or designing a wheel-chair, what matters is not the importance of the object of study or the complexity of the conditions which influence its execution. What matters is not the size of the reward or the significance of the individual concerned. What matters is the intensity and the integrity with which the essentials have been explored and expressed. What drives is that creative urge.'

In 1982, Milner Gray gave an interview to Jane Lott of *Design* magazine. She recorded:

'Modern times find him still very much in the thick of things, still working, still on committees (such as that presiding over the new 20 pence and £1 coins from the Royal Mint). He has said "I think it is a good sign that we're moving on from pop; it was the lowest common denominator – and it's no good telling me that all men are equal. They're not. I can appreciate my superiors in design."

'His patriotism is practical: "We should be able to make all sorts of things and not afford them ourselves. Until we do, we *can't* afford them ourselves. Similarly, the Swiss make amazing ships' engines, and don't have a navy. They don't grow cocoa beans either."

'"I'm very optimistic," says Gray, "the role of design in the world is growing stronger. The need to understand it is being appreciated by engineers more." Yet he has fears at the spectre of his profession seduced by contemporary aids: "If graphic designers lose the capacity to draw lettering, just as if product designers lose the ability to draw, it would be disastrous. Just look at Leonardo's notebooks – drawing is basic to thinking."[48]

In October 1983, a plaque was put up at the Cock Tavern in Fleet Street to commemorate the meetings that led to the founding of the Society of Industrial Artists and Designers in 1930. *The City Recorder* reported:

'The Host Group became the owner of a "Designer Pub" recently when Sir Hugh

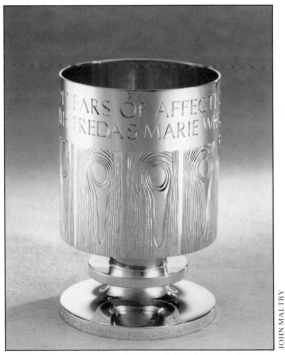

JOHN MALTBY

Presentation beaker designed by Gray in 1970.

Casson, President of the Royal Academy, unveiled a plaque at one of Fleet Street's oldest public houses.

'The green and white plaque commemorates the first meeting of the Society of Industrial Artists and Designers (SIAD) at The Cock Tavern, in Fleet Street, in 1929.

'Sixteen former Presidents of the Society attended the unveiling, including Mr Milner Gray, the only surviving member from that original pub meeting. It was Mr Gray (83), a former President of the SIAD, who designed the special plaque.

'Addressing the meeting, Mr Gray said it seemed a far cry to 1929 when the founder members met at The Cock with the dual aim of enjoying refreshment and discussing the need for a professional association. He also presented the pub with a bound copy of the SIAD's early history for display on the premises . . .'[49]

Afterwards Milner Gray remarked that he couldn't remember whether or not there had been sawdust on the floor at the time of the original meeting in The Cock Tavern and received a card through the post from Sir Brian Batsford saying only, 'Yes, there was sawdust on the floor'.

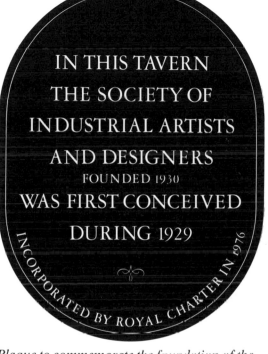

TONY CLEAL

Plaque to commemorate the foundation of the SIAD at the Cock Tavern, Fleet Street.

1984

So much that has not changed

The year 1984, in which this book was written, was made ominous to us all in George Orwell's projection of life as it had seemed, in 1948, that it might become. However, the effect of change has not proved easy to predict and, for designers, even big developments in computer-aided design and computer graphics have not really changed the nature of industrial design. They have only, in certain circumstances, speeded up the process. The words about design have changed over the years, but the activity has remained much the same as it was in 1921 when it was first practised by Bassett-Gray.

The idealism that has always been apparent in art schools, especially after the war and even in the anarchic 1960s and early 1970s, has been rationalised in the face of the need to earn a living in a time of recession. But a fundamental question remains: to what degree should individual young designers stand out for high principles or adapt their ideas to commercially viable taste?

There can be only personal answers to this continuing dilemma. Young designers, embroiled in the simple business of responding to practical needs, may feel they are missing out on the more creative and revolutionary ideas current at that time. Colleges of art and design in Britain are chiefly concerned with problem solving, and it could therefore be that there is a tendency for the designer to become less able to develop entirely new approaches. Commercialism, also, can inhibit a designer's freedom to experiment: in trying to be practical, the baby of creativity may tend to be thrown out with the bath water of free expression.

In Italy, for example, designers have a creative energy that owes nothing to mere problem solving or market research, and designers in, for example, 'The Memphis Group' have gone beyond the comparatively simple process of analysing the problem and providing solutions to fit the stated need. They achieve innovatory ideas that could not be reached by any defined and straightforward approach. In this they have been almost as near to fine art as Graham Sutherland's and Clive Gardiner's work for Bassett-Gray.

This type of design may not always be commercially viable for mass markets, yet it creates a visual imagery for design that is recognised world-wide. This leads the way by creating its own market and is a vital activity if stagnation is to be avoided. The design world must remain vigorous and even idealistic in these terms of it will settle for easy cynicism and devious politics.

Bassett-Gray, Industrial Design Partnership and Design Research Unit, Milner Gray's three design practices, managed to maintain a good balance between commercial practicality and ideal innovation. Each July, young designers leave the art schools full of ideas. It is the aim of this biography of Milner Gray to inspire them, even in the face of all the opposition their work will meet, to believe that the struggle for high standards can be worth while.

Appendix A

SIGNPOSTING STANDARD COLOURS
AND SHAPES AT THE FESTIVAL OF
BRITAIN

1   Yellow (circle)
    For Traffic directional signs, circulation etc.
    a) Main route
    b) Preferred route within buildings
    c) Exit
    d) Emergency Exit (incorporating also
        emergency colour)

2   Green and white (per pale with diabolo)
    For Intelligence: General Services
    a) Enquiries, information
    b) Bookstall, publications

3   Light blue and white (hexagon)
    For Hygiene
    a) Lavatories: Women
    b) Lavatories: Men

4   Magenta (lozenge)
    For Refreshment
    a) Restaurant
    b) Buffet
    c) Sweets and chocolates
    d) Ice creams
    e) Cigarettes and tobacco

5   Scarlet and White (per pale)
    For Communications
    a) Post Office

6   Red (triangle)
    For Emergency Services
    a) Fire fighting equipment

Further signs, not as yet agreed upon, such as telegrams, telephones (group 5), bars (group 4) or first aid posts (group 3/6) could easily be added and would fall into line by the adoption of the colour and shape of their appropriate groups. Equally, further variations of colour and shape could be found to cover different generic purposes, such as entertainment (cinema and concert hall) or travel (bus or train departure points, travel offices, etc.) and be added within the general structure of this plan.

Notes

1 'The Beginnings of the SIA – Design in the Thirties': talk at the Victoria & Albert Museum, 8 November 1979.
2 *Art and Industry*, November 1950, p. 180.
3 Notes for Arts Club dinner on 11 October 1979.
4 Dorothy McCall (1952) *When That I Was*. London, Faber & Faber.
5 Notes for Arts Club dinner on 11 October 1979.
6 Ibid.
7 James Holland (1980 *Minerva at Fifty – The Jubilee History of the Society of Industrial Artists and Designers, 1930 to 1980*. Westerham, Kent, Hurtwood Publications.
8 Notes for Arts Club dinner on 11 October 1979.
9 In *Minerva at Fifty*.
10 Ibid.
11 The Ministry of Information Report, INF 1/132, pt. A., of 6 December 1941 contains a letter from Bloxham to Royds saying, 'There has been quite a talk at the RIO's [Regional Information Officers] conference on Friday to the effect that some of our shows are wrongly labelled exhibitions. I feel that the word is applied very wrongly and leads to too much expectation. The Division agrees with me on this.' Created as a Division in 1943.
12 Known as the 'War Artists Advisory Bureau'.
13 According to Milner Gray in *Designers in Britain*, vol. 3, pp. 17–18.
14 Pick '. . . held a high post for a time, but failed to hit it off with the minister, Duff Cooper, or his top civil servants' according to Noel Carrington (*Industrial Design in Britain*, 1976, London, p. 132). Christian Barman noted in an obituary that Pick's idea and experience of management was 'centralised and dictatorial'. The young MoI, presumably, could not accommodate such individualism.
15 Referred to in a 'secret' note (INF 1/33, 8.12.1939) as necessitating authority for additional staff. This note also refers to 'overcoming the present German superiority in photographic publicity'.
16 *Advertisers Weekly*, 25 November 1943.
17 Letter from A. W. Waterfield, in INF 1/132, pt. A, 18.12.1950. The DOT technical exhibition staff were, however, so employed.
18 Which made him ineligible for salaried employment.
19 At the rate of £8 8s (£8.40p) (INF 1/132, pt. A).
20 This presumably refers to his immediate pre-war experience.
21 No relation to Frank Pick.
22 These details taken from a statements of payments to outside designers and architects used by exhibitions branch between January and April 1943 (INF 1/133).
23 Misha Black (1950) *Exhibition Design*. London.
24 Julian Trevelyan *Indigo Days*, p. 186.
25 Milner Gray in conversation with Judith Ann Freeman.
26 It seems that Bloxham may have disturbed the status quo somewhat.
27 'Coal-Mining in Regent Street' (1942) *Architectural Review*, December.
28 'The Dramatic Principle in Exhibition Technique', *Art and Industry*, no. 194.
29 Peter Austen (1946) op. cit., p. 212.
30 Fiona MacCarthy (1972) *All Things Bright and Beautiful*. London.
31 In *Minerva at Fifty*.
32 Thesis on British Graphic Design, with special reference to government publicity, 1939–51.
33 *The Practice of Design* (1946) Lund Humphries, London.
34 See also Milner Gray and Ronald Armstrong (1962) *Lettering for Architects and Designers*. London, B. T. Batsford.
35 *Art News and Review*, 27 January 1951.
36 In *Minerva at Fifty*.
37 *A Tonic to the Nation* (1975) London, Thames and Hudson.
38 Interview with Jasper Grinling, 25 April 1984.
39 Weidenfeld and Nicolson, London, 1966.
40 Hutchinson, London 1949, Peregrine Books, London, 1963.
41 Routledge and Kegan Paul, London, 1973.
42 In *Minerva at Fifty*.
43 B. T. Batsford, London, 1962.
44 Michael Middleton, (1966) *Group Practice in Design*, London, The Architectural Press.
45 'Fitness for What Purpose?' in *Design*, 29 August 1974, and also in *The Black Papers on Design*. (1983), Oxford, Pergamon Press.
46 *Visual*, Vol. 4, no. 2, 1966.
47 *The Sunday Telegraph* magazine no. 105, April, p. 11.
48 Interview by Jane Lott, *Design*, June 1982.
49 *The City Recorder*, 13 October 1983.

Milner Connorton Gray

CBE, RDI, PPSIAD, AGI, M.Inst.Pkg., Hon.Dr RCA, Hon.DA. Manc.

PERSONAL DETAILS

Born Blackheath, London – 8th October, 1899. Son of the late Archbibald Campbell Gray and the late Katherine May Gray, née Hart, of Blackheath and Eynsford, Kent. Educated privately and Colfe Grammar School, Lewisham. Studied painting, engraving and design at Goldsmiths' College, London University. Served 1917–19 in 19th London Regt. and Royal Engineers attached first Camouflage Unit. Married 12th July 1934, Gnade Osborne-Pratt, no children.

HONOURS AND PROFESSIONAL QUALIFICATIONS

1930	Member of Society of Industrial Artists
1938	Royal Designer for Industry
1945	Fellow of Society of Industrial Artists
1947	Member Institute of Packaging
1950	Member Alliance Graphique Internationale
1955	Design Medal Society of Industrial Artists and Designers
1957	Diploma 10th Triennale di Milano
1957	Design Centre Award
1963	Commander of the Order of the British Empire
1963	Honorary Fellow of the Royal College of Art
1965	Honorary Associate Manchester College of Art and Design
1971	Senior Fellow, Royal College of Art
1977	The Queen's Silver Jubilee Medal
1979	Honorary Doctor, Royal College of Art
1979	Honorary Fellow Society of Typographic Designers

PUBLIC APPOINTMENTS

1929–30	Member Pre-formation Committee, Society of Industrial Artists
1930–32	Founder Member of Council SIA (now SIAD)
1932–40	Honorary Secretary SIA; 1940–43 Vice President and Vice Chairman of Council; 1943–49 President. 1966–67 President (second term)
1932–40	Member Visiting Staff Goldsmiths' College, London University; Chelsea School of Art; Reimann School of Art and Design
1935–38	Member of Council Design and Industries Association
1937	Delegate Leader SIA/PORZA Assembly Paris International Exhibition (22–25 October 1937)
1937–40	Principal Sir John Cass School of Arts and Crafts
1938–50	Member MARS Group (British Section CIAM)
1938–39	Chairman SIA Working Party to consider the setting of examinations in design and the granting of qualifying diplomas
1939–40	Member Visiting Staff Royal College of Art
1940–44	Head of Ministry of Information Exhibitions Branch and Principal Design Adviser
1943–45	Chairman Drafting Committee SIA Memorandum to Board of Education on 'The Training of Designers for Industry'.
1944–45	Council Member The Central Institute of Art and Design (liaison representative to Ministry of Works, Standards Committee, Directorate of Post-War Planning)

1944–45	Consultant Exhibition Designer Council for the Encouragement of Music and the Arts (now The Arts Council of Great Britain)
1944–45	External Examiner to the four principal Scottish Art Colleges at Edinburgh, Glasgow, Dundee and Aberdeen
1945–46	Member of Board of Governors, Central School of Arts and Crafts
1947–52	Member Ministry of Education Advisory Committee on Art Examinations
1949	British Council Lecture Tour — Australia and New Zealand
1949–55	Adviser BBC Schools Broadcasts 'Looking at Things'
1952–	Member Royal Mint Advisory Committee
1954–60	Chairman SIA Education Committee
1955–57	Master Faculty of Royal Designers for Industry
1955–57	Vice President Royal Society of Arts (Member of Council 1959–65)
1955–64	Member Packaging Advisory Council, Printing and Allied Trades Research Association
1955	UK Delegate Speaker International Design Conference, Halsingborg
1956	Member Formation Committee International Council of Societies of Industrial Design (ICSID)
1957	Chairman Panel of Judges for the first Council of Industrial Design Awards for 'Designs of the Year'
1958–68	Chairman/Member SIA International Relations Board
1959–69	Member National Advisory Council on Art Education
1959–60	Chairman SIA Drafting Committee for 'Syllabus for the Study of Professional Practice in Commercial and Industrial Design'
1959	Delegate to ICSID Conference, Stockholm
1959–	Council Member, Artists General Benevolent Institution
1961–63	Chairman SIAD Trust Fund Committee
1963	Master Art Workers' Guild
1963–67	Member of Council, The Royal College of Art
1963–67	Member CoID/GPO Stamp Advisory Committee
1963–71	British President, Alliance Graphique Internationale
1965	Delegate European Packaging Conference, Copenhagen
1966–67	President SIAD (second term)
1968	Leader SIAD delegation to International Council of Graphic Design Associations (ICO GRADA) 3rd General Assembly and Congress, Eindhoven
1969	Member Committee appointed jointly by The British Academy and the Royal Commission for the Exhibition of 1851 to 'Review the Activities of The British School of Rome'.
1970	Delegate Speaker, Design Council Conference on 'Corporate Identity – its Organisation and Management'
1972	Conference delegate to Design Council Conference on 'The Management of Design for the European Markets'
1972–77	Member Standing Joint Committee SIAD/Design Council
1973–76	Chairman, SIAD Charter Working Party leading to the grant of a Royal Charter to the Society

PROFESSIONAL APPOINTMENTS AND PRINCIPAL WORKS

1922–35	Founder and Senior Partner in multi-discipline design group practice under title 'Bassett-Gray Group of Artists and Writers'
1932	Designer, Promotional scheme – symbol, poster, press advertisements for launch of London Building Centre
1933	Joint Design Co-ordinator, Commercial Art Section, Advertising and Marketing Exhibition, Olympia, London
1933	Exhibited printed textile designs, Exhibition of British Industrial Art, Dorland Hall, London
1933–34	Design Consultant to E. Brain and Co. Ltd. (Foley China)
1933–34	Design Consultant to A. J. Wilkinson and Co. (Royal Staffordshire Pottery)
1935–40	Senior Partner in re-organised group practice under title 'Industrial Design Partnership'
1936–40	Mural designs and decorative features for Kardomah Cafes, London, Birmingham, Manchester.
1937	Designer, Christie-Tyler hammock principle domestic chairs
1938	Section Designer, MARS Exhibition of Modern Architecture, London
1939	Designer, murals and decorations Maritime and Fine Woollens Sections, British Pavilion, World Fair, New York
1940–44	Principal Exhibition Designer and Head of Exhibitions Branch, Ministry of Information: Designer 'London Pride', first MoI exhibition, Charing Cross Underground Station (1940)
1945	Designer, CEMA 'Design at Home' exhibition, National Gallery, London
1945–	Founder Partner, Design Research Unit
1945–48	Design of Emblems for the Ministry of Agriculture and Fisheries, for the Export Credits Guarantee Department, and rendering of the Royal Coat of Arms for the Council of Industrial Design (CoID)
1946	Designer, CoID Reception area, 'Britain Can Make It' exhibition, Victoria and Albert Museum, London: exhibited project designs for an improved taxicab and cooker
1946	Designer, symbol, house style and package designs for Rolex Watch Company SA, Geneva
1946–66	Design Consultant to Ilford Ltd. for Corporate Identity Programme: Offices, showrooms, exhibitions, packaging
1947	Designer, Ascot Gold Cup
1947–50	Design Consultant to D and J Wellby Ltd., for Silverware
1947–48	Designer, Aluminium Holloware for Midland Metal Spinning Co
1948	Designer, 'Design at Work' exhibition of the work of Members of the Faculty of Royal Designers for Industry, Royal Academy of Arts, London
1948–51	Joint Designer, South Bank Signposting, 'Festival of Britain'
1949–50	Design Consultant to Austin Reed Ltd. for Corporate Identity scheme.

1949–55	Design Consultant to Courage and Co. for Corporate Identity and Public House Identification Programmes.
1949–55	Designed trade-marks for Allen and Hanbury, Austin Reed, Courage and Co., Pyrex, Rolex, Scottish Furniture Manufacturers Association
1950	Designer, Milk Bottle Filling and Capping Machine for UD Engineering Co. Ltd
1951	Designer, Engraved Glass Screen at entrance to Royal Box, Royal Festival Hall, London
1952–53	Designer, Rendering of Royal Coat of Arms, Crown and Royal Cipher for Coronation Decorations and Souvenirs, for the Council of Industrial Design
1953–69	Design Consultant to W. and A. Gilbey/International Distillers and Vintners Ltd
1954–55	Design Consultant to Tate and Lyle Limited
1955–57	Joint Design Consultant to the De La Rue Group of Companies
1955–65	Design Consultant to James Joblings Ltd, for 'Pyrex' oven-to-table glassware
1956–70	Design Consultant to the Watney-Mann Group of Companies for Corporate Identity and Public House Identification Programmes
1957–60	Joint Co-ordinating Designer for the public areas in the P. and O. Orient liner 'Oriana': designer of the Ship's badge
1961–	Design Consultant to Royal Mint for coin inscriptions and coin and medal packaging
1962	Design, for glass engraving and print, of armorial bearings for Birmingham Chamber of Commerce
1962–63	Design Consultant to British Railways Board for British Rail Corporate Design Programme: Chairman Joint BR/DRU Corporate Identity Working Party, 1963–64
1963	Design and modelling of armorial bearings for Central Electricity Generating Board
1966–70	Design Consultant to Imperial Chemical Industries for Corporate Identity Programme
1967–72	Design Consultant to British Aluminium Company for Corporate Identity Programme
1970	Design of Armorial Bearings and Common Seal for the Post Office
1972	Design of Badge for the Balmoral Estate Ranger Service
1973–75	Design Consultant to Courage and Co. for re-evaluation and up-dating of their public house identification
1976	Design of Official Emblem for the Queen's Silver Jubilee for use on street decorations and souvenirs
1976–77	Design Consultant to British Rail for station decorations for the Queen's Silver Jubilee

PUBLICATIONS, LECTURES, PAPERS

1928	'The Initial Conception', Publicity Club of London, 26 January.
1933	Package Design', *Packaging*, August.
1934	'Shape, Design and Colour', Commercial Art and Industry, October.

1939 'The History and Development of Packaging', Royal Society of Arts, London, 8 March. *RSA Journal* no. 4511.

1944 'Standards not Standardisation', Design and Industries Association, Royal Society, London 12 May.

1946 *The Practice of Design* (contributor), London, Lund Humphries.

1946 'The Design of Sales Packaging', Council of Industrial Design Conference, London, November.

1949 'The Industrial Designer and Consumer Goods', Royal Society of Arts, London, 19 January. *RSA Journal* no. 4792.

1949 'Industrial Design in Great Britain', lectures and broadcasts in Australia and New Zealand for The British Council, 23 February–13 April. Report 21 April.

1950 'Functional Design', Domestic Equipment, March.

1951 'A Century of Commercial Design', *Designers in Britain*, no. 3. London, Allan Wingate.

1951 'Never been twenty-one before', *SIA Journal*, April.

1952 'The Work of Robin Day', *Art and Industry*, May.

1952 'Exhibitions – In or Out', *Art and Industry*, October.

1953 'In the Case of Art v Advertising', *Penrose Annual*, vol. 47.

1953 'Presentation', Royal College of Art, 5 October.

1954 'Design Training', Leader *SIA Journal*, December.

1955 *Package Design* (author), New York, Studio Publications.

1955 'The Creative Urge', Royal Society of Arts, London, 26 October. *RSA Journal* no. 4965.

1955 'The Designer's Dilemma', International Design Congress, Halsingborg.

1955 'Halsingborg Puts Out More Flags', *RSA Journal*, July.

1956 'A Brave Lot o' String', Double Crown Club, 8 February. *Advertising Review* no. 7.

1956 'Retrospect to Prospect – Design for the Changing Ways of Life', DESIGN no. 89, May.

1957 'Design for Selling', *Financial Times*, 21 January.

1959 'The Family Pack', *Emballages*, Zurich, Graphis Press.

1959 'Packaging Progress', *RSA Journal* no. 5037.

1960 'Public House Style', DESIGN no. 139.

1960 'A Designer's Approach to Image Planning', Packaging Association of Canada Conference, Toronto, 9 March.

1961 'Professional Practice', SIA Education Conference, Royal Society of Arts, London, 9 January.

1961 'The Fair Oriana', Municipal College, Bournemouth, 5 February.

1961 'Man – Problem Solver', 11th International Design Conference, Aspen, Colorado, USA, 18–24 June.

1961 'Two Leaves from Aspen', DESIGN no. 155, November.

1962 *Lettering for Architects and Designers* (joint author with

Ronald Armstrong), London, Batsford.

1963 'The Changing Years', Master's Address, Art Workers' Guild, 11 January.

1963 'The Image Makers', SIAD, NE Region, Leeds, 5 March.

1964 'The Design Process', Institute of Export, Newcastle-on-Tyne, 10 February.

1966 'Retrospect and Prospect', Women's Advertising Club of London, 10 May.

1967 'The Oldest and Youngest Professions', Society of Industrial Artists and Designers, Minerva Dinner, 30 November.

1968 'The Corporate Image', Institute of Public Relations, NW Area Group, Manchester, 16 January.

1968 'Another Skill', National Association of Engravers and Die-Sinkers, London, 30 May.

1968 'The Frontiers of Time', *The Designer*, June.

1968 'The Frontiers of Perception', Chairman's Summary Address, SIAD Annual Conference, Chipping Camden, 9 June.

1968 'The Price and the Value', SIAD Presidential Address, Nash House, London, 25 September. *The Designer*, November.

1968 'Accident or Design', Society of Industrial Artists and Designers, Minerva Dinner, 26 November.

1969 'Reminiscences of a Designer', Arts Club, London, 5 November.

1970 'Development of a Corporate Design Programme', Design Council, Corporate Identity Conference, London.

1973 'Fifty Years On', Advertising Creative Circle, London, 5 June.

1979 Response on behalf of Doctors Honoris Causa, Royal College of Art, 6 July.

1979 'I think I remember', Arts Club, London, 1 November.

1979 'Design in the Thirties – the Beginnings of the SIAD', a Lecture sponsored jointly by the Arts Council and the Victoria and Albert Museum, 8 November.

REFERENCES IN BOOKS AND PERIODICALS

1927 'The Work of the Bassett-Gray Studio', *Commercial Art*, 27 December.

1933 'Advertising and Marketing Exhibition, Olympia, *Gebrauchgraphick*, Berlin, September.

1934 'Weingarten Mural', *Design for Today*, London, April.

1935 'Industry in the Windtunnel', *Design for Today*, London, July.

1936 'Industrial Design Partnership', *Packaging Review*, July.

1940 *The Times*, p. 9, 29 March.

1940 Julian Trevelyan, *Indigo Days*, p. 186.

1941 'London Pride – a Rare Piece of Display', *Display*, March.

1942 Christian Barman, 'Frank Pick', *Architectural Review*, January.

1942 *The Times*, 12, 17 and 19 October.

1942 'Coal Mining in Regents Street', *Architectural Review*, December.

1943 'Dig for Victory', *Architects' Journal*, 11 March.

1943 'The Wartime Exhibition',

Architectural Review, October.

1943 *Advertisers Weekly*, 25 November.

1943 *The Times*, 10 March, 8 June.

1944 *The Times*, 6 January.

1945 'Design at Home Exhibition',
Architects' Journal, 23 August.

1945 'Design in Everyday Things',
Picture Post, 6 January.

1947 *Designers in Britain*, no. 1. Also
references in nos. 2, 3, 4, 5, 6, 7
(the last three published by André
Deutsch, London).

1947 John Gloag, *English Tradition in
Design*, London, King Penguin.

1947 Noel Carrington, *British
Achievement in Design*, London,
Pilot Press.

1948 'RDI Exhibition at Burlington
House', *Architects' Journal*, 21
October.

1949 'Milner Gray – a Profile',
Packaging Review, no. 38,
October.

1950 Misha Black, *Exhibition Design*,
London, p. 12.

1950 *The Domestic Equipment Trader*,
vol. 1, no. 5, March.

1950 'Designer Milner Gray', *Art and
Industry*, London, November.

1950 Charles Rosner, 'Milner Gray',
Graphis no. 68. Zurich, Graphis
Press.

1950 'Cockerel for Courage', DESIGN,
July.

1950 *Art and Industry*, p. 180,
November.

1951 *Art News and Review*, 27 January.

1954 Herbert Read, *Art and Industry*,
New York, Horizon Press.

1955 'Brewers House Style',
Architectural Review, December.

1955 'A Quarter Century of Decision',

The Ambassador, no. 12.

1956 'Milner Gray, London'.
Gebrauchsgraphick no. 2, Berlin.

1956 *Advertising and the Artist*, Ashley
Havinden, London, p. 12.

1957 *Display Presentation*, Beverley
Pick, London, p. 12.

1957 'The Art of Packaging', *The
Ambassador*, no. 12.

1957 'The Art of Showing Off',
DESIGN no. 106, October.

1958 'DRU', *Stile Industria*, no. 19, p.
27, Milan.

1960 'SS Oriana, a survey', *The
Ambassador*, no. 12.

1961 'Design Research Unit',
Arkitekten 14, 4 July,
Kobenhaven.

1962 John Lewis, *Printed Ephemera*,
Ipswich, W. S. Cowell.

1962 *Graphis*, no. 104, p. 595

1963 'British Rail Uniforms', DESIGN
no. 171, p. 65, March.

1963 'How they do it in Britain',
Industrial Design, May. Whitney
Publications Inc., USA.

1965 'Milner Gray, CBE', *House and
Garden*, August.

1966 'Milner Gray – a Profile', *Visual*,
the Ilford Journal, vol. 4, no. 2.

1967 Michael Middleton, *Group
Practice in Design*, London, The
Architectural Press.

1968 Gordon Russell, *Designers Trade*,
pp. 234, 256, London, Allen and
Unwin.

1969 John and Avril Blake, *The
Practical Idealists*. London, Lund
Humphries.

1969 'Jubilee Celebrations for the Men
from DRU', DESIGN, no. 245,
May.

1969	'The Black and Gray Revolution', *The Sunday Times Magazine*, March.
1970	Communication by Design, James Pilditch, McGraw Hill.
1970	'DRU: 25 Years of Design for Industry', *Graphis*, no. 147. Zurich, Graphis Press.
1972	Fiona MacCarthy, *All Things Bright and Beautiful: Design in Britain, 1930 to Today*, p. 112. London, Allen and Unwin.
1975	*A Tonic to the Nation*. London, Thames & Hudson.
1976	Noel Carrington, *Industrial Design in Britain*, p. 132.
1976	*Design Systems for Corporations*, May.
1976	Nos. A2 and B2, British Rail and I.C.I. reviewed. The CoComas Committee for Business Administration and Management, Tokyo.
1980	'Sutherland leaves behind an affectionate memento', *Sunday Telegraph magazine*.
1980	'Milner Gray by Graham Sutherland', *The Designer*, April.
1980	James Holland, *Minerva at Fifty*, Westerham, Kent, Hurtwood Publications.
1981	'Still Achieving, Still Pursuing', *The Drawing Paper*, p. 8, August. London, Woodpecker Publications.
1982	'Interview – Drawing People Together', DESIGN, p. 25, June.
1982	Roger Berthoud, *Graham Sutherland*.
1983	*The City Recorder*, 13 October.

Acknowledgements

First of all Milner Gray, himself, who supplied the material for this book and was wholly constructive in his corrections and comments on the draft manuscript; James Holland and the Society of Industrial Artists and Designers for letting me quote freely from *Minerva at Fifty*; Fiona MacCarthy for a quotation from *All Things Bright and Beautiful, Design in Britain 1830 to Today*; Judith Ann Freeman for permission to use, as Chapter 3 and part of Chapter 4, a portion of her thesis on 'British Graphic Design, with special reference to Government Publicity, 1939–51'; Jasper Grinling, Director of Corporate Affairs, Grand Metropolitan Hotels, for information about the work done by Milner Gray for W. & A. Gilbey Ltd.; Gerald Barney, June Fraser and Stuart Rose for memories of working for Design Research Unit; Lady Black for letting me quote from Sir Misha's article 'Fitness for What Purpose'; Michael Middleton and The Architectural Press for permission to quote from *Group Practice in Design*; *The Sunday Telegraph* magazine for permission to print their report on Graham Sutherland's portrait of Milner Gray; and *Design* magazine for permission to quote from sundry articles.